Blues Discovery: Reaching Across the Divide

(2nd Revised Edition)

Matthew Ismail

Dost Publishing

Dost Publishing version
Copyright 2023
Matthew Ismail
All rights reserved

2nd Revised edition of *Blues Discovery: Reaching Across the Divide* (2011)

https://www.dostpublishing.co/

To the memory of Ray Flerlage Fred Mendelsohn Samuel Charters, and Bob Koester.

PREFACE (2023)

Blues Discovery was something of a forgotten project. I wrote this book when I was in my late 20s as an extension of my old passion for the blues. I spent many wonderful hours talking to my friend Roger Brown about his youthful discovery of blues and the bluesmen whose music he loved so much. Writing the book was a labor of love. I wrote *Blues Discovery* in my spare time when I was working in North Carolina in the late 1990s and not long after I had completed an MA in Modern European Intellectual History at the University of Chicago. I had previously completed MAs in Humanities at the University of Minnesota and in Islamic History at Ohio State University, so I had some research and writing background on which to draw. Yet, when I took a job in the Emirate of Abu Dhabi in the United Arab Emirates in 1999, the book got lost in the fray.

I lived in Sharjah, United Arab Emirates and Cairo, Egypt, for twelve years. My children were born in Abu Dhabi and Dubai, but I also traveled widely in Eastern and Western Europe and made trips to Turkey, Thailand, India, Morocco, South Africa, Namibia, and Botswana. While we were overseas I also wrote and published a biography of the British Museum Egyptologist Sir E. A. Wallis Budge called *Wallis Budge: Magic and Mummies in London and Cairo* (Rev Ed., Dost Publishing, 2021).

When I moved back to the States in the wake of Egypt's Revolution in 2011 and began to think about new projects, I remembered the fun I'd had interviewing Roger Brown, Ray Flerlage, Bob Koester and Samuel Charters about fifteen years before and decided to get back to *Blues Discovery*. When I finally located the three and a half inch floppy disks (on which the text had been stored) amidst the loads of stuff I had left in storage in 1999 before leaving for the UAE, I wasn't even certain that my laptop would be able to read the text, which had been written on Word 95.

After some tech-savvy assistance from a colleague at work, however, I was able to salvage most of what I had written. The bibliography and discography were gone so I had to rework what I could remember of the books I had consulted; I wasn't able to track the various old Yazoo, Biograph and Library of Congress records I'd consulted during the writing because I just didn't know what had become of them. Those who know the music will be able to identify which albums I was listening to, anyway.

And as for the cassettes on which I had recorded the interviews...I have no idea what's become of them, unfortunately. The quotes in the text are all that remains of them.

I've reread *Blues Discovery*, of course, and I am aware that the history sections are now out of date, so I deleted them. The interviews, and the stories based on those interviews, are the core of the book, so the history section is not essential. This book is a series of stories about young Americans in an age of segregation and desegregation reaching across the social and political divide to the musicians whose music was so important to them.

I have also been able to correct some errors from the previous editions with the assistance of Roger Brown, George Mitchell, and Gerd Wieben.

In addition to corrections, I have also added a couple of appendices, which are reproductions of blog posts I did based on conversations with Roger Brown in December of 2011.

Since speaking to the informants whose stories are the center of the book in the 1990s, some things have changed. Roger Brown has retired from teaching German at the University of New Hampshire. Ray Flerlage, whom I enjoyed meeting so much, died in 2002 at the age of 87. Fred Mendelsohn died in 2000. Samuel Charters died in 2015. Bob Koester of Delmark Records and Jazz Record Mart died in 2021. It was a great pleasure and an honor to speak to all of them. May they rest in peace.

Table of Contents

PREFACE (2023)	iv
CHAPTER I: ROGER BROWN & GEORGE MITCHELL	1
CHAPTER II: ROGER & GEORGE, DECEMBER 1961 & SPRING 1962	10
CHAPTER III: ROGER & GEORGE, TENNESSEE, SUMMER 1962	30
CHAPTER IV: ROGER & GEORGE, PEG, BIG JOE AND BUDDY IN 1963	43
CHAPTER V: ROGER AND GEORGE, LATE 60S, NEW ORLEANS, ATLANTA, L.A.	56
CHAPTER VI: ROGER & GEORGE, ROBERT JR. LOCKWOOD	68
CHAPTER VII: RAY FLERLAGE, "OUTRAGEOUS AND WEIRD"	76
CHAPTER VIII: RAY FLERLAGE AND PHOTOGRAPHY	84
CHAPTER IX: BOB KOESTER & DELMARK RECORDS	98
CHAPTER XI: BOB KOESTER, JUNIOR WELLS, AND MAGIC SAM	118
CHAPTER XII: AN INTERVIEW WITH SAMUEL B. CHARTERS (4/28/1996)	130
APPENDIX A	165
APPENDIX B	169
APPENDIX C	173
SELECT BIBLIOGRAPHY	177
ABOUT THE AUTHOR	180

CHAPTER I: ROGER BROWN & GEORGE MITCHELL

An 18th century New Hampshire farm house is about as unlikely a place to hear the blues as one could imagine. But if you'd stood outside one particular New Hampshire farm house in late August of 1995 you would have heard nothing but the blues. As Roger Brown and I talked about his and George Mitchell's youthful discovery of the down-home blues in Atlanta in the 1950s and 1960s, we would take breaks to blast the house with everything from his reel-to-reel field recordings of Will Shade and Charlie Burse to a rollicking R & B set by Sonny Boy #2 (also, incidentally, the name of Roger's basset hound). We listened to Son House's intense Library of Congress sessions of 1941, and laughed as we listened to the interview an earnest Roger attempted to conduct with a less-than-earnest Furry Lewis in Memphis in 1970 [see Appendix A]. At some point, Roger even made me take the drop-the-needle exam from the blues class he teaches at the University of New Hampshire, which I was (thankfully!) able to pass.

It was Roger, a friend of the family and colleague of my father's, who introduced me to blues back in the early 1980s, and it was the LPs he'd bought for his blues class at Hiram College in the early 70s that were my introduction to the music. Twenty years after he'd left Hiram, we talked blues and listened to music for three days in New Hampshire. His story began not in Hiram, however, but in Atlanta, the city in which Roger and his old buddy George Mitchell were born in 1944.

*

In 1955, across the segregated city of Atlanta, flowed a black music called rhythm and blues that ignored all of the boundaries that American society had set up to keep black and white people separate. As played by Mississippians such as Sonny Boy Williamson, Robert Nighthawk, or Little Walter, R & B was the child of the down-home blues of the Delta--a child of the country that had moved into the cities.

R & B was not a music emanating from the Deep South any longer, but primarily a music of the urban ghettos of the North. If Muddy and Howlin' Wolf both stopped in Memphis on their way north to Chicago, it was in Chicago that they made their homes. Chicago, New York and Detroit after 1945 provided southern blacks with a new environment to create a new music. There was a new prosperity for many urban blacks after the War, and starting in the late 1940s, there were radio stations such as WDIA in Memphis (with B.B. King as a DJ) that played R & B for, of and by the black communities. If network radio excluded black music and culture, WDIA lived for it.

By 1955, most large urban areas had at least one R & B station aimed at a black audience, but something else was also happening in the larger culture that was intimately related to the developments in R & B. Chuck Berry had hit the charts in 1955 with "Maybelline," an R & B version of a country tune made (at Muddy Water's suggestion) at Chess Records in Chicago. Little Richard had hit, similarly, with "Lucille," and Elvis Presley had covered Arthur Crudup's 1946 R & B hit "That's Alright" for Sun Records in Memphis in 1954. The Memphis-based Jerry Lee Lewis was presenting a shocked America the spectacle of a wild, twisting, country-bred white man playing piano much in the style of black barrelhousers. Rockin' rhythm and blues, also called rock and roll, was a hit everywhere in America, and Variety called 1955 "the year that rhythm and blues took over the pop field."

Rock and roll was a total break from the style of white popular music of the pre-rock era: Perry Como and Tin Pan Alley were eons away from Chuck, Richard, Jerry Lee and Elvis. But rock was not eons away from R & B, and R & B was in large measure the city stepchild of a down-home country relation called the blues. For some music listeners, the down-home country relation was discovered behind its urban descendants out of a curiosity to hear the roots of it all. For young teenagers Roger Brown and George Mitchell, listening to the R & B station WAOK in Atlanta ignited a passion for black music that led them, eventually, back to the down-home blues.

Roger Brown happened across the radio station WAOK quite by accident. He was in his room in suburban Atlanta spinning the dial on his radio after school, hoping that something interesting would come out. He wasn't looking for R & B, but once he hit it, Roger was hooked. He'd turned to the Pop station, WEEK, in the past, but it was so frothy that he even found it wanting as a sixth grader!

But WAOK was something else, and he began to dig in with a passion. He remembers, almost forty years later, that WAOK was organized as a Hit Parade. There were some songs on the station which were hits week after week, such as "Walkin' By Myself" by Jimmy Rogers. There were other songs, such as Muddy Waters' "Rock Me," that Roger went home every day hoping to hear. The songs were far from the schmaltz of Johnny Mathis et al, and they had a sense of earthiness that was entirely lacking in pop music. Elmore James' 1950s R & B hit "Dust My Broom," for instance, which was a tune played regularly on WAOK, was a screeching electrified cover of a Robert Johnson song of 1936. James' rowdy slide guitar and high, rough, vocal combine to create a dance tune of great energy and passion:

> I'm gon' get up soon in the mornin', I believe I'll dust my broom. (x2)
> I done quit the best gal I'm lovin', now my friends can get my room.
> I'm gonna write a letter, telephone every town I know. (x2)
> If I don't find her in West Helena, she's in East Monroe, I know.
> I don't want no woman wants every downtown man she meets.(x2)
> Man, she's a no-good doney; they shouldn't allow her on the street.
> I believe, I believe my time ain't long. (x2)
> I've got to leave my baby, and break up my happy home.

Along with Elmore James, the station churned out the hits by the likes of Chuck Willis, Ruth Brown, Little Willie Littlefield, Otis Rush, Bobby Bland, Big Mama Thornton, Jimmy Reed, Slim Harpo, Sonny Boy Williamson, and such popular groups such as the Coasters and the Midnighters. The pianist Piano Red, who was something of an old-timer, had a regular afternoon show that Roger listened to after school, and he remembers well Red's gleeful and knowing annihilation of the English language, including such grammar-twisters as "I hate to left you, but I do have to went!"

And not only was the music great, but the DJs were fascinating. The head DJ was a white man named Daddy Sears, a cool guy who knew the music backward and forward and dished it out in a warm and appreciative style that made him a favorite in the city. There was also a guy called Alley Cat Pat and the sexy-voiced "Dream Girl," but they played back seat to Daddy Sears.

WAOK was a great source of music, and it was also something that bound together a few of the young teenagers into a tight group. Roger's friend George Mitchell, who would later produce some very fine blues albums and organize nationally renowned folk festivals in Atlanta, also spun that dial and made the same discovery, as did a few other close friends, such as Jim Lester and Jack Boozer. They would turn around in their desks at school and ask if the others had heard Sonny Boy or Big Mama last night, and young as they may have been, they were extremely enthusiastic.

Roger recalls that the first 45 he bought was Little Richard's "Lucille" in sixth grade (prompting his mother to exclaim in despair: "What have you done to my Roger!"), a piece of rockin' R & B if ever there was one, and a purchase which showed his musical direction very nicely. "Please, Please, Please" by James Brown was his second purchase. His third purchase began to move back in time to the hits behind the founders of rock and soul: after hearing Arthur Crudup's low-down "Mean Ole Frisco" on WAOK, he made his way down to a place called Central Records on Decatur Street to invest a bit of his allowance in a 45.

Central Records became Roger and George's favorite place to go after they discovered it sometime around 1956 or '57. The store was in the Five Points area of Downtown, about six miles from Roger's house in Druid Hills, and it was smack in the middle of the main drag of black Atlanta. The store was owned by a white guy named Bill Barrow who knew the R & B scene in Atlanta in a way probably only equaled by Daddy Sears among Atlanta whites. Daddy Sears would even mention Barrow often on his program. Roger would take the trolley downtown, which took about half an hour, and would go right to the store. There was a bus stop near the entrance to Central Records which meant there was always a mob outside.

Roger remembers, all these years later, arriving at the store after a few years of going there and seeing Barrow's beautiful wife for the first time. Barrow introduced them and told his wife a story that illustrates, succinctly, Roger's entry into the blues: "I remember when Roger first came in here. He slapped a quarter on the counter [making a gesture suggesting that Roger could barely reach it] and said 'Gimme some blues! I want some blues!'" They all laughed, but Roger admits it wasn't far from the truth.

Bill Barrow was a show in himself. He would stand behind the counter spinning disks for customers, speakers blaring, grabbing a 45 and slapping it on the turntable with a great flourish, playing a few bars for a potential buyer and hoping to draw a few other buyers at the same time. He was prone to put on a particularly hot number and dance behind the counter saying (using a bit of black lingo): "This is the worst blues out! This is the worst blues out!" And he sold them like hotcakes.

There were other guys who sold at Central Records who Roger remembers. There was a very knowledgeable black man who asked Roger if he'd ever heard Blind Lemon Jefferson's "'Lectric Chair Blues" (1928), showing a fine understanding of the blues long before his own day. There was another guy there whom Roger recalls, as well. He was a chubby white guy with long hair slicked back and a cigarette dangling from one corner of his mouth. Roger went in to buy a 45, and he came back to the counter with Little Willie Littlefield's "Ruby, Ruby." When the guy gave him his change, he looked Roger seriously in the eye and said in a low, appreciative, voice: "You're really livin', Daddy!"

If Central was Roger and George's favorite place, there were other mainstream stores over in the Peach Street area to which they'd also go. Where Central was loud, funky and gritty, the others were the sorts of places that one found in plazas. But these places, even though they sold mostly classical and the sort of white folk music that Roger and George didn't really like, also had the good stuff. George went to a place down by the Lowes-Grant Theater and picked up a couple of Big Bill Broonzy LPs that were among the first down-home blues that the two of them heard. When he brought them up to the counter, the salesman was impressed and said to George: "You know how to separate the good from the bad, don't you buddy?" There were sympathetic souls even where they didn't expect to find them.

The fact is, of course, that these teenagers didn't have enough money to support their habit, and as teenagers a wont to do, there was a certain amount of shoplifting. Roger remembers vividly going to a plaza store with George and finding a Folkways LP that had Blind Lemon, Yank Rachel, Rabbit Brown, and then a bunch of Creole and cowboy stuff on the outer bands. They didn't have the money to buy the LP, and since they really only wanted what was on the inner bands, George hatched a plot to make the LP small enough to rip-off without losing the good stuff: he sneaked back to the listening booth with an Exacto knife and a lighter and hoped that he could carve off the outer part of the disc and reduce it to 45 size. After long work which scarred the LP horribly, George gave up and they left without the swag.

Not that long afterward the two of them returned to the record store to try again. They encountered two problems on this visit, both of which they brought to the attention of the woman behind the counter. First, a record in which they were interested was in a wrong jacket ("It was in the wrong jacket because we put it in the wrong jacket!"), and she said that this could easily be remedied. Then, with a theatrical flourish, George whipped out the scarred Folkways LP and said, feigned horror in his voice: "And then, look at this!" She was considerably more irritated by this turn of events, but did nothing. They still had no LP. Roger went back a few weeks later, however, and asked her if she'd cleared up the problem, and by this time she'd had enough: "I'll give you that!" she cried. Roger finally got the LP, and George was mad at Roger, in the end, for making off with his goods.

Roger remembers very well that a friend of theirs named Tommy Bland had a father from Statesboro, Georgia, the locale of Blind Willie McTell's "Statesboro Blues" of 1927. Tommy's father remembered Blind Willie, knew him in fact, and Roger thus knew, long before research told us so in the 1970s, that McTell was from Thompson, Georgia not Statesboro, where he used to visit quite often. It was this same Tommy Bland who came by to visit him with a friend one day about 1959 or 1960, and Roger pointed out proudly that he had in his collection the Riverside Blind Lemon LP and the Folkways LP that they'd tried to "alter." Bland was a real blues buff, but his friend was not at all interested. When they arrived, Roger played the fantastic "Poor Boy" by Ramblin' Thomas, and Roger told Tommy's friend that it would grow on him. The friend looked dubious, and said: "It would take a long time for that to grow on me..." But the next time Roger saw Tommy, Tommy said that the guy was hooked. It was Roger's first convert.

*

In 1959, while they were still limited to contemporary R & B, a book was released that changed the musical horizons of the two fifteen year-olds dramatically: *The Country Blues*, by Samuel Charters, which was released with an accompanying LP. The boys happened upon the book not because they were looking for books on down-home blues: in fact, they had no idea that such a thing existed. These were a couple of kids who were R & B fans, and they would never have imagined that there was an older music related to R & B that might be of interest to them. Charters' book described the blues recording industry of the 1920s, the great variety of country blues artists, the locations of the recording and the backgrounds of the musicians. To Roger and George, the whole idea of "country blues" was a revelation that immediately caught their attention, and has held it for the following forty years.

Having read *The Country Blues*, Roger immediately got hold of the LP and called up George as soon as it arrived. Roger held the phone's receiver up to the record player and the first drop of the needle netted (a coincidence full of portents) Peg Leg Howell's "Low-Down Rounder Blues" (1928). He said to George over the phone: "You are listening to Peg Leg Howell!" and this was the first either of them had heard of Peg, whom they would later discover in his house in an Atlanta slum. Sleepy John Estes' 1938 tune "Special Agent," also on the LP, knocked them off their feet. That Estes would perform this tune for them on the porch of a house across the street from his Brownsville shack in 1963 was beyond their dreams--the notion that someone who recorded in the 1920s and 30s could even be alive in

1959 was an impossibility to the fifteen year-olds! The earthiness of the music, the subdued passion, immediately hooked both of them. Having heard some down-home blues, says Roger, "We couldn't get our hands on it fast enough!"

While a huge amount of country blues has become available to purchasers since the middle 1960s, this was not so in 1959. One could not jettison R & B immediately and rush to the blues, since there really wasn't that much blues to be had: besides Charters, there were the Folkways LPs of Leadbelly and the Story of Jazz series; a couple of Broonzy LPs; Fred Ramsey's recordings of Horace Sprott, which amounted more to field hollers than to blues; and Riverside's *The Country Blues*. Roger picked up *The Country Blues of John Lee Hooker* in 1959, and perhaps saw something new in Muddy's earlier recordings, such as "Can't Be Satisfied" (1948) on the *Best of Muddy Waters* LP that he had also bought, but that was about it.

Neither Roger nor George were, incidentally, interested in "folk music" of the Woody Guthrie or Weavers variety. They only lament the effect of Guthrie and Alan Lomax on Leadbelly, which issued in bizarre numbers such as "The Bourgeois Blues"! They were decidedly not "folkniks." As a result, Roger was immediately repelled by the "folksy" Josh White, a black member of the Greenwich Village folk scene, and was truly amazed, in the mid-1960s, when Buddy Moss told him that White had once performed straight blues. Nothing could be farther from the earthiness of the blues than the Josh White of the 1950s and 60s. For George and Roger, the music had to be the authentic blues to be of interest.

It was also in 1959 that Roger had an encounter in Atlanta that he wishes now he'd been old and experienced enough to follow up on. It was summer, 1959, and the fifteen year-old Roger was working pushing a concessions cart long hours at a farmers market near Atlanta. One afternoon, at the end of a long day when there wasn't much business, he was pushing the cart and singing "Mean Ole Frisco" to pass the time. He ran across a big, muscular, middle-aged black man sitting on a bench who said to him: "Boy, what're you doin' singin' the blues?" Roger responded that he loved blues, and the man leaned over to him and asked, confidentially: "You ever heard of Peg Leg Howell?" To this Roger replied enthusiastically, saying that he loved Peg Leg Howell, and mentioned the "Low-down Rounder Blues" from the Charters LP, which was all he knew.

Looking back, he kicks himself for not asking the man why he brought up Peg in particular, since that might have allowed them to catch him a few years before they did so in 1963, by which time he was badly deteriorated in health. Again, it was inconceivable to the young teenager that someone who'd recorded in the 1920s could still be alive, and it never occurred to him to see if Peg (to say nothing of McTell!) still lived in town, right under his very nose.

Perhaps the great turning point in their young blues enthusiasts' lives was when they listened to Willie Borum's Bluesville/Prestige LP of 1961 called *Introducing Memphis Willie B.*, with notes and production by Samuel Charters, himself. In reading the liner notes, Roger and George noted the amazing fact that Will Shade, a Memphis associate of Borum's in the Memphis Jug Band days of the 1920s, was still alive and living in a ramshackle tenement off Beale Street in Memphis. Still living!? They could hardly believe that it was possible-- but there it was. Shade, the founder, organizer and heart of the Memphis Jug Band, whose 1928 tune "Stealin', Stealin'" was on the Charters LP, was still alive, at least as recently as the issue of this Willie Borum LP.

Was it possible that Shade was still there in Memphis, and that two white high school kids from Atlanta could actually speak to him? If Charters could do it, why couldn't they? This idea struck them hard--they wanted to find Shade, and they were going to use their next vacation to do it. These were not your usual teenage boys, worrying about sports and girls to the exclusion of all else: these two had a sense of adventure, and they were going to make a road trip to Memphis to find out what they could about their musical idols.

This interest in meeting Shade was not, however, celebrity worship or mass-media fantasy created in Hollywood and New York. This was a couple of people with a passion for blues, a passion for the music that was a large part of their musical and intellectual lives. They weren't just going through some adolescent phase, but were making a discovery: they'd found kindred spirits in the blues, and they were going to make contact with them if at all possible.

CHAPTER II: ROGER & GEORGE, DECEMBER 1961 & SPRING 1962

It was Christmas vacation, 1961, and Roger and George were ready for a Memphis road trip. They did no planning for the trip beyond calling George's aunt in Memphis, and they left Atlanta with no camera, no tape recorder and only the money from their allowances to finance the trip. At age seventeen, the two were young and inexperienced, and they left Atlanta with only the haziest of ideas what they would do when they got there: they were going to Memphis to look for Will Shade on Beale, based on Charters' aside on the Willie B. LP that it was Will Shade who put him on to Borum. That was it. They were by no means confident that they would find Shade, the information was so thin.

It is important to note that the two of them knew of the Memphis music scene only the little bit that appeared on the Charters LPs and a couple of others: they knew the Memphis Jug Band's "Stealin', Stealin'," Cannon's Jug Stompers' "Walk Right In," and a few other tunes. This was all before the blues Bible of Godrich and Dixon, so they did not know the names of songs or personnel to ask about or to request. The trip was handicapped not only by their inexperience, but by the lack of the reissues and histories that were later available.

So, the two of them loaded up Roger's silver and white '57 Chevy and took off. The weather was cold, but never a problem, and the journey took them uneventfully across Georgia and Alabama into Tennessee. When they finally arrived in Memphis and made their way to George's aunt's house, they were ready to go that next morning.

*

Stories about the rediscovery of great bluesmen are often fairly labyrinthine affairs. The wild goose chase that was the search for Son House is a good example. The search began in New York City, and the searchers went down to Mississippi to look for House where he was last known to be. On arrival in Mississippi, they were eventually told that he had moved to Rochester, New York some years before! So, back they went to Rochester, where they found the musician working as a janitor. The journey was 4,000 miles and sixteen states long, and they heard many, many conflicting stories from informants before they finally came across House.

Roger and George had more to go on than did those who were seeking people who hadn't been heard from for thirty or forty years, but the trip was in a similar vein. They were setting out to find a musician who had been active in the recording scene thirty or so years before, and all they knew was that he'd not yet died a few years previously. Where he lived was only vague known, and the two high school kids from suburban Atlanta had absolutely no experience with field work. They were working from pure moxie, not from training in ethnomusicology. So when they left the aunt's home and drove down to Beale Street the first morning after their arrival, it was with the intention to spend the entire day searching for Shade.

The story moves very quickly. Roger and George parked down on Fourth and Beale, near W. C. Handy Park, and went in to a drugstore on the corner. They asked the pharmacist, an older white man, if he knew Will Shade and he said no, "But ask Charlie--he's been on this corner for fifty years." As Roger and George walked back to the front of the store, someone else said, "Ask Whiskey. He knows more than Charlie." They walked outside, and sure enough, there stood Whiskey, a tall, thin, old man with a pinched face. They asked Whiskey, who was about fifty and average height, if he knew Will Shade, and Whiskey turned on his heel and practically bolted across Fourth Street with the boys following.

Whiskey then led them down an alley to a beat-up old tenement building and up the dingiest staircase that Roger had ever seen. Like most such staircases, it smelled of urine. As they began to mount the stairs, Roger remembers very well their increased excitement-- something seemed to be happening. He then remembers the quick rising of adrenalin when they heard, in this horrible place, the sweet twinkle of a tenor guitar coming from somewhere upstairs. Whiskey led them up to the door from which the music was coming, knocked a couple of quick knocks, and yelled in his sharp, clipped fashion: "Son Brimmer! Someone to see you!"

The door soon opened and there stood Will Shade, himself. He was shirtless and looked to be about sixty-five. Roger and George stood there in the hallway, speechless and amazed, and Shade just smiled a friendly smile, stuck out his big hand and said: "Shade's my name."

One of the two managed to say: "We've come all the way from Atlanta to find you." They were still amazed at their luck, since it had been about five minutes from the time that they'd parked the car to the time they'd shaken Son Brimmer's hand, but they were totally unprepared for what followed. Shade turned around and said to another man in the room: "They're from Atlanta, Charlie. Let's play 'em the 'Kansas City Blues'!" Shade then stood by Charlie (as yet with no last name for them), and the two of them pounded out Jim Jackson's old classic in a performance that Roger remembers as one of the highpoints of his life.

Roger was delirious--incredulous. He was just floating with pleasure. He never thought he would actually see and hear such a thing. "Shade was just all over that harp with those great big hands of his, and [Charlie] Burse was just beatin' the hell out of that tenor guitar." This really knocked them down. He later figured out that the Memphis Jug Band had recorded "Kansas City Blues" in Atlanta in 1927, and that Shade was playing the song in honor of the fact that they had come from Atlanta. It was obvious that Will and Charlie felt no discomfort or awkwardness in dealing with the boys, and there was no need the break the ice or break down barriers of mistrust.

In fact, as Roger recalls, they seemed to be very pleased that these guys had come all the way from Atlanta to see them and listen to them play. The fact was that they were forgotten men living in poverty in a slum, and their lives were no doubt both harsh and often dull. The apartment was one room with a Murphy bed, and Roger later saw in the apartment a rack of raw fish that had been taken from the river. Will later told them that he had been grateful to them for not expressing any disgust, because he knew it was a bad odor, but there was nothing else he could do, poor as he was. No matter what their profound musical talents and sensibilities, Will and Charlie were living in pretty depressing straights; this visit by the boys was not just a reaffirmation, of sorts, of the talents that set them apart from the majority of people and made them special, but a break in the routine. Will and Charlie were flattered that they were thus remembered, and though they'd talked to other researchers (Charters, Oliver, Dick

Allen) previously, this was probably a different feel--the youth of the two Atlantans, as well as their personable friendliness, must have been a pleasure for them.

After the song, they found out that Will and Charlie were going down to the Peabody Hotel, as they had for many years at Christmas, to play for tips--they had been rehearsing when Roger and George arrived. Roger and George offered to give them a ride down to the Peabody and then pick them up later, and the two gladly assented. They all went down to the car, and on the way they chatted about music--Roger remembers asking them about Ralph Peer, and that Shade was reeling-off things about the Memphis Jug Band's shifting personnel and about songs such as "State of Tennessee Blues" and "Oh, Ambulance Man" that were news to them. At one point, George turned to Charlie and asked: "Are you Charlie Burse?" since they'd read about him somewhere in connection with the Memphis Jug Band. It was here that they got a little taste of Burses's ego, as he puffed up with pride on being recognized.

They all went in to the Peabody together, and Roger and George watched the men perform for a while. They didn't play blues for this crowd, of course, but Roger and George were just happy to watch them play. Burse was in his entertaining mode, and he was doing the duck walk as he played, and Will played his oil can bass. They were making a hit with the crowd, and a white businessman came up to Will and arranged for them to play later that day for a private party. Roger and George arranged to meet them at the party to drive them home. When they returned to pick up Will and Charlie later, they found that the two had left early because Will's bum leg was bothering him. They reconnected at Will's apartment later.

Roger cannot remember now which night it was, but he remembers that the ukulele player Laura Dukes came over to the apartment to pay a visit, and that, as an diminutive woman in her forties, the elderly Shade felt obliged to flirt with her. His leg bothered him so much that he had trouble holding a job, and it was hurting him that night. When Dukes offered to massage it, Shade smiled and with a glint in his eye, he said to her: "You'd have to rub me all over!" She just smiled back at him and ignored his dirty old man's humor.

The next day after the Peabody trip, George bought a cheap "Brownie" camera. They took a few pictures and then Will took them over to see Willie Borum. Borum was not as easy to deal with as were Will and Charlie since he had a recording contract with Charters, he was very scrupulous about honoring it, and his wife obviously disliked Will's influence on him. She no doubt had visions of drunken debauchery as the immediate result of hooking up with the likes of Shade, and her worries were probably justified. When Will asked Borum to play something, he said he could not record except for Charters, and they had to assure him that there would be no recording, only playing.

It was then that the experience was intensified yet more. Roger and George, thrilled that they'd gotten past the mistrustful Mrs. Burse, now heard a few great sets performed by Will and Charlie. There was much Golden Harvest Sherry for Will, bought with Roger and George's allowance money, and the others were drinking their share, too. Will's common-law wife, Jennie Mae Clayton, joined in and belted out a few verses during their session. She'd sung a few times for the Memphis Jug Band in their memorable 1927 session, including "State of Tennessee Blues," and her high-pitched howl was still in pretty good shape for a seventy year-old woman (she was older than Will) who was not in very good health.

Though Jennie Mae had only one lung, she was bumming cigarettes off of them the whole time they were in Memphis. She was no shrinking violet. She sang "Oh Ambulance Man" at the session, and Roger and George thought for a long time that it was she who'd sung the song at the Memphis Jug Band sessions when it was originally recorded, as well as other tunes they heard without personnel attached. When they found out later that it was Hattie Hart who'd sung them, they were very sorry that they hadn't been able to ask the now dead Will and Charlie about her, because she is both a very obscure figure, and one of Roger's favorite female vocalists.

Neighbors seemed to drift in and out of Will and Jennie Mae's apartment at will, some of them dancing to the music, laughing, joking and enjoying the party atmosphere. This was standard practice for the blues scene, but was a new phenomenon to a couple of white kids from Druid Hills.

The pictures from the session with Willie B. are revealing. There is one picture that shows two very young looking, clean-cut, white kids, standing side by side, smiling the polite smiles of upper middle class teenagers. Before them in the picture are Will Shade and Willie B., also seeming to be enjoying themselves, laughing and holding their instruments. The picture is over-exposed, and the whiteness of the boys is intensified. They look callow and pleasant and very happy.

And they were surely happy. Willie B. was still in very good musical shape, having just cut an album, and his playing on the guitar and harp was fantastic.

At some point in the trip, Will took the boys to see Furry Lewis. As with their quick trip to find Will, they found Furry quickly because Will just took them to his door and knocked. Furry was hospitable, and made a very sober impression on them, but he could not play for them because his guitar was in hock. They just visited with him, and Furry, at this point, was displaying his formal pose of being a very sincere, up-standing and sober individual. If one is acquainted with Furry's music--his meditative blues, his pained vocals, his melancholy lyrics, and the commiseration of his "talking" guitar--it was easy to accept this public version of himself. When Furry began to know them better, however, his rowdy, drinking and decidedly not sober side came out in full bloom.

Another trip was made to Gus Cannon's apartment, but he had moved since the last time Will had been there. When they found out where he did live, they did not find him home--but looking through the window, they saw a banjo and a jug, and figured this must be the place!

At one point in the trip, Will wanted to play something for Roger and George on guitar, but his guitar, like Furry's, was in hock. Now, as Will knew, down the alley from him, in another run-down tenement building, lived the noted blues guitarist Bo Carter (born Armenter Chatmon c. 1899), who had just had a stroke. Will suggested that they go down the alley and ask Carter if they could borrow his instrument, and this seemed to be a good plan all around, since Roger and George would also get to meet Bo Carter.

They found Carter in pretty bad shape. He could speak rather haltingly, but could not play at all. He told Roger and George a bit about the bluesmen he had known, mentioning Leroy Carr, for instance, and reminisced for them as best he could. But Will was only interested in the guitar, which hung diagonally on the wall of the apartment. This was to prove a problem. Though Carter was willing that Will should borrow his guitar, his son-in-law, who had since come into the room, was not. When Will asked, the son-in-law refused angrily, and there was tension, suddenly, in the air. Will did not give up immediately, saying, sheepishly, that he would leave a deposit, but the son-in-law was firm, and nothing could turn him from his refusal. Roger says that the anger was so intense that it was a bit scary.

Finally, they gave up hope of gaining the loan of the guitar and left. Roger and George were convinced, by this point, that the son-in-law resented these white people coming into his house and trying to rip him off, or something. As they passed through the door, however, the situation was offered in the plain light of day. The son-in-law called to them and said in a harsh tone: "Y'all come back. Don't bring that son of a bitch wich ya!"

They could hardly believe it: Will was hated and distrusted so much that he wasn't even trusted with a loan if he left a deposit! This was news. This was amazing. But their regard for Will did not die that easily, even though a bit of skepticism had crept in. A later story, gained from Robert Lockwood, Jr., would tarnish this god still more-- but that in good time. George went back to Carter's apartment the next day with his camera, to conclude this episode, but his wife said that it was not appropriate that Carter should be photographed, since he was preparing to meet his maker. He died soon afterwards.

*

The first trip to Memphis, in December, 1961, was a great success in some ways, less so in others. The brief trip allowed Roger and George to meet Will and Jennie Mae, Charlie, Willie B., Gus, and Furry. They'd not just seen them at a concert or exchanged a few guarded pleasantries with them, as one is wont to do with "celebrities," but rather had shared their lives with them for a few days. They'd seen firsthand how the musicians lived, what place the music occupied in their lives, and the setting in which the Memphis Jug Band's music lived naturally: in a tenement with neighbors dancing and laughing in the background. And they'd at least managed to take a few pictures.

Of course, they kicked themselves mercilessly for not bringing a tape recorder, and had they known that everyone's guitars would be in hock, they'd have tried to bring one. And had they had access to Godrich and Dixon, they would have asked many questions that only Will could answer about the Memphis Jug Band and which went unasked before he died in 1965.

One topic that was broached in December, 1961, was a possible concert. Roger and George had it in their minds that they might be able to get these musicians together in Atlanta for a Memphis blues concert, and had brought it up while still in Memphis. The concert was called "The Revival of the Blues," and it never took place.

*

The concert idea had come into Roger and George's heads while they were listening, spell-bound, to Will, Charlie and Willie B. perform. Why not get these guys on stage, a non-profit performance that would showcase their talents to all who were interested? In addition to being a cultural event to gain publicity for this downhome music, it would be a way of reviving Will and Charlie's moribund musical careers. The two felt profound gratitude to Will and company for being so generous and hospitable to them, and wanted to pay them back in any way possible. The idea of a concert back home in Atlanta appealed to both of them, and they assumed that they would be able to find a certain number of people willing to attend the performance.

When they brought the idea up with the musicians, they were all for it. Will and Charlie were willing and enthusiastic, though there was an immediate problem: Charlie's ego. Charlie was a splendid musician, but an extremely vain and egotistical individual. Will must have learned how to deal with him long before, since they'd been friends for nearly forty years.

Charlie, it seemed, was not willing simply to be a part of the show. He must be the featured performer, the main attraction, or he would not participate. This man, who made his living painting houses, was unable to take part unless he was set apart from the others as the superior attraction, and he began to throw a temper tantrum on the spot that was worthy of a five year old. Roger and George were, suffice it to say, surprised by his behavior. They loved his music so much that it was hard to believe that he could be such a childish individual.

Roger and George decided, quickly, to take Charlie into the hall outside Will's apartment and reason with him. They talked the matter over with Charlie, who would not budge, and finally solved the problem by promising that Charlie would be paid $5 more than all of the others. This appearance of superiority was quite sufficient, and he went back inside completely satisfied. As long as his superiority was recognized, he was fine. "Charlie Burse," says Roger in 1995, "The most irrepressible person I've ever met. No question about it."

With the idea in hand, Roger and George returned to Atlanta with high hopes for a Memphis blues concert. They worked hard on the idea, and eventually set the date for Friday, April 6th, 1962.

One of the first things that they did was have George design a poster announcing "The Revival of the Blues." The design chosen was basically a high-jacking of the cover of the 1961 Robert Johnson Columbia LP that shows a man sitting in a chair, his long legs before him, hunched over a guitar and looking at the floor. They took this poster over to a printing facility in East Point, and also had some tickets printed up.

Roger remembers well going to a local radio station, WGKA, and buying some spots for the concert there. WGKA was mostly a classical music station, but it also had a folk hour. They knew that the most important announcer was a man named Lee Nance, who had a deep, elegant and mellifluous voice that poured out of the radio as he announced the next piece of fine classical music. They went to the station and walked in to look for Nance, and came upon a man in a small office wearing a white tee shirt and with a cigarette in the corner of his mouth. Taking him for the janitor, they asked the man if he knew where Lee Nance was. The man looked at them and responded in a beautiful, deep, voice: "I'm Lee Nance." Nance, at any rate, agreed to sell them some spots on his show, and they left, highly amused by the incongruity of Nance's appearance and his radio persona.

All of the planning for this concert came out of their own money, not from their parents, and the strain was tremendous. To finance the concert, Roger and George had initially thought of trying to get fifty people to commit a certain amount of money and guarantee an audience, but this proved to be difficult. While talking to Gene Hall, a math teacher at their school, about the project, Hall suggested to them that they contact a local amateur jazz musician that he knew named Mark Wilkerson, who may be able to help them. The teacher also suggested that they go to Morehouse College to try to get some help.

Wilkerson was a white jazz musician who worked a day job, but Roger says he was a splendid musician. He was also an enthusiast for authentic folk music, and a member of a musical group called The Traditional Jazz Society of Greater Atlanta (kin to clubs elsewhere such as the St. Louis Jazz Club to which Bob Koester belonged). Wilkerson was sympathetic to their ideals, and he even contacted his friend John Pennington, the star reporter for the *Atlanta Journal*, and had him come over to his house to meet Roger and George and discuss their project.

Pennington, as it turned out, was very much in sympathy with Roger and George's taste in folk music: it had to be a pure product--a music for, of, and by the folk community of which it was a part. Pennington railed against a recent Odetta concert he had seen at Morehouse, in which Odetta, a black American folk singer, sang Irish ballads! He'd as soon listen to an Irish bard sing a lowdown blues. Roger was told later by Fred Ramsey that Louis Armstrong had wittily defined folk music to him as "What folks listen to," and this seems to catch the spirit of the thing quite nicely. Odetta was definitely not their cup of tea, and she got thrown in with Josh White and others that Roger and George disliked as merely commercial. Pennington was impressed enough to want to write an article for the *Journal* on this "revival of the blues," and George and Roger agreed.

After talking to Wilkerson and Pennington, at any rate, they went to Morehouse and talked to Marvin Anderson, who was president of the student body at the time. He was very friendly and cooperative, and they were encouraged that Anderson was confident that Morehouse could come up with the money to cover the minimum of $400 that would be incurred in paying the musicians and in expenses. They assumed that this would guarantee both a minimal audience for the musicians and get back their own initial investments, which would amount to about $150. As cooperative as Anderson was, there were problems on the way from the college bureaucracy. Roger remembers, specifically, that a Mr. Nix, who was the business manager, was very uncooperative, and that he basically would not find a way to free up the money that the students had all agreed upon. The concert was strangled by red tape in the cradle, but they kept on trying.

Pennington, in the meantime, called Roger's house to get some background on Roger for the article. Pennington's article was one that contained a certain amount of misconception about the two boys. He wanted to write an article glorifying Roger and George as good boys, displaying qualities (as he put it in the article) "the opposite of juvenile delinquency--of juvenile initiative and enterprise." He regarded them as good boys because they rejected evil and degenerate rock and roll, and because they were doing something worthwhile with themselves, not being hoodlums.

This was in the period when "juvenile delinquency" was a big mass-media issue, and bad boys such as James Dean and Marlon Brando were routinely trashed for representing the worst in teenage rebellion. For Pennington, Roger and George were clean-cut, serious minded, and trying to be good Americans. These boys will amount to something, mark my word, rings all through the article. The two did nothing to disabuse Pennington of his ideas about them, but Roger admits that the picture was a false one. He knew them not at all. In fact, says Roger, "We had plenty to be ashamed of!" Though they were not fond of rock, they had plenty of wild, drunken parties that featured the "gutbucket-est" blues that they could find. There were drunken evenings with Forest City Joe, and drunken evenings with Blind Lemon. Roger and George ran with the wildest crowd that affluent Druid Hills had to offer. "We were wilder than shit-house rats," he says, though they were careful to be discreet because they came from respectable families. Blues and booze were the common denominators of their high school days, and if Pennington had any inkling of this, he didn't let on at all in the article.

Pennington, in fact, got much information on Roger from a family friend. Pennington called Roger's house to talk to Roger before he wrote the article, and Roger's parents were having a bridge party. When the phone rang, the "dummy" of the hand, and man named Griff, went to answer the phone. When he found it was for Roger, he went back and told the others that it was their son. They said he was not in, and Griff went back to the other room and did not return for some time. When he finally returned, Roger's father, assuming that Griff had been chatting with one of Roger's buddies, said to him: "You make a friend, Griff?" It was Pennington, however, and he had grilled Griff all he could to get the low-down on Roger and George. Perhaps the 4-H flavor of the piece was the product of Griff's polite praises of his friend's son, to some extent.

This activity was in the midst of the failure to secure the Morehouse backing, and Roger and George were struggling to keep the concert alive. There was a promoter in town, one who had brought Joan Baez to Atlanta not too long before (a major coup in 1962), who got wind of the concert and decided he wanted a piece of the action. His motivations seemed more territorial than helpful, and when they went to talk to him they found that he was really a very sleazy type a guy. This meeting also had the effect of alienating Mark Wilkerson, for whom the project suddenly lost its purity. It was no longer these virtuous American teenagers doing something admirable and industrious, but something that promised to become a crude money-making venture for this money-grubbing promoter. As it turned out, the promoter's overtures came to nothing, anyway, and they were still on the verge of losing the concert.

In the meantime, Roger, in March 1962, in the midst of all of this planning and running in circles, had his wisdom teeth out. He was incapacitated by the operation, but not so much that he didn't worry and continue to work to save the concert. In the middle of March, they tried one last gamble. Roger's father, a doctor, knew a man named Frank Bradshaw in Atlanta who was originally from Memphis. Bradshaw owned the largest Chevrolet dealership in Atlanta; his parents back in Memphis also owned a Chevy dealership and Bradshaw's father was a patient of Roger's father. Roger had a plan that was not very well thought out: they would ask his father to talk to his patient in Memphis, secure from them the loan of a car from their dealership there, and use the car to get around in Memphis. George left on the bus to Memphis with his friend Jack Boozer, and Roger approached his father about the car on the Memphis end.

They hit a rather nasty snag at this point. Though in visiting the bed-bound Roger he'd just generously offered to buy "several" concert tickets himself, he said that he did not know the Memphis Bradshaws well enough to ask favors of them. With George and Jack already on the way to Memphis, things looked bad. When George arrived in Memphis he went to the car dealership and asked about the car, and to his surprise the people said they had no idea what he was talking about. George and Jack contacted Will and Jennie Mae, but little was solved. One thing that George recalled from the trip was that Jennie Mae, with one lung left and in very poor health, kept bumming cigarettes from Jack Boozer, who was called "Mr. Jackson" by the black Memphites (apparently because of being introduced to them as "Jack"). They returned to Atlanta with the concert still in question.

All the while, as they planned and spent what money they'd saved from allowances, Roger and George were receiving letters from Memphis, both from Laura Dukes and Will Shade. Shade's letter of January 30, 1962, the earliest one, closes with a request for drinking money that was to continue for some time. He begins by saying [sic.] "Dear Mr. Brown. I receive your letter and Jinnie Mae and I was More glad to heare from you all." He continues by telling them, apparently in response to a question, that "Tee Wee Blackman is dead and I am sorry Because We Was Verry good friend and also Jinnie Mae Claton is still Living ho put out Bob Lee Junior Blues and the state of tennessee Blues." He tells Roger where to look for an example of one of his old contracts with Ralph Peer, and thanks him for a picture of him and Jennie Mae. Then he gets down to business:

"Listen Mr. Brown We hafter have a Gantee on What Wee Will Make Week they Wont Come On no tip Basis or [?] Basis they Wont a Gantee...We Was Base On sixty [?] But they Wonter go for that I dont no if You are Charging Buy the seat or not I Wont You to send me What Will You all pay Pur Man by the week Write me at Once and let Me Know I Wont to no Could We get your tips like We Was...I dont Wont you to dissapoint Me like You dont me to dissapoint You I Wont you to let know to Weeks head of time so I can get every thing totheger [sic] Listen Mr. Mitchell I Wont you to send me the price of some milk I Will pay You and One pay you When I hit atlanta ether when You come here. From your Truly Will Shade"

Unable to send Will any money and busy with the planning and school, the two made no response. In a letter dated March 23, 1962, as things went to hell around them, Roger received the following advice from Laura Dukes:

"Mr. roger Brown I got your letter and was glad to hear from all of you don't let Will Shade know that I wrote to you all I want you to tell your friend Mitchell don't give any of them to much to drink Until they get ready to Come home I sure like my Uke I will be there if nothing happens so that is all I hope to see all of you the 6 of April. Laura Dukes"

As if in response, Shade sent another letter asking for drinking money, this one more insistent, and his coded request this time was the one about money to buy shoes. For an impoverished alcoholic, a request for drinking money is no laughing matter. The letter was written in another hand for him (and with more proper punctuation and spelling) and dated March 22, 1962. After a polite opening of "Dear Sir--" and some other pleasantries written by the penman, Shade says:

"I received the money $2.00 for the guitar strings. I got them right away. But you did not send any money to get me some shoes like I ask you and that is very important because I need them very bad. I do not want to wait until you come up here to get them. I want you to advance me some money out of my own check because you know you'll pay me off and you can't lose. Please send me the money at once so I can get the shoes and be wearing them to break them in before you get here. I hate to worry you so much but this has to be done. On account of a necessity please don't turn me down on this..."

After telling Roger and George how nice their poster for the concert is, he says that Jennie Mae would also like to make the trip, but needs to be paid, too. "She wouldn't want to come way there just for the ride." Then back to the money for the shoes:

"I forgot to tell you how much money I need. I need $20.00 so please not let me down. Be sure to send Charlie Burse one of the posters. Tell Brown, Jackson [Boozer] + Mitchell that Jennie Mae says hello and that she has that song ready, and don't drink too much milk. Please answer at once--Shoe Money--From Will Shades Rear 225 So. Fourth St."

Not deterred by the lack of twenties coming in the mail for himself, Will then sent a note on behalf of Furry on March 24, 1962:

"Dear Mr. Brown and Mr. Mitchel I am Writing You to let You Know about Furry Lewis he need a little expence Money it something thing He Need Verry bad he Wont to Know Could he get ten Dollars expence On this end so he can take care thing On this end What Need through We Wont hafter balder You about enthing When You come. We are going to have every thing redy When You Come Thank You all"

In the meantime, with all of the planning, writing of letters, and attempts to save the concert apparently at an end, the Pennington article appeared in his column in the *Journal* under the title "Concert Backfires: Atlanta Teeners' Quest for Blues Finds Oldsters."

"Two Atlanta high school students, tired of rock 'n' roll and nourishing a new interest in the beginning of jazz, not only found [the musicians], they almost put them on the stage in a concert here. / They failed; this is the story of a "Revival of the Blues" that might have been. It involves a youthful pursuit that cost the two a hard $150 cash between them, but paid off in an experience of a lifetime."

The article detailed their journey, the musicians involved, the adventures and misadventures. It also included a certain appreciation of the music, quoting some lines from blues songs and trying to display some of the gritty and earthy attraction of the music. The article told of the problems of gaining funding, the disappointments of failed planning, and concluded:

"The long and short of it was that, one week before concert time, George and Roger had to sit down and write their Memphis musicians that the whole thing was off. The boys were good finders of musicians, their rejection of rock 'n' roll was admirable; so was their courage and initiative in going off to Memphis' Beale Street to find the old-time singers. But they were not businessmen."

The article was something of which both Roger and George were very proud, but it was also intricately enmeshed with the fact of their failure.

Nonetheless, when Frank Bradshaw, the Atlanta Chevy dealer, saw the Pennington article announcing the failure of the concert, he offered, in their last gasp of hope, to have the concert on his Chevrolet lot. He saw no problem in letting the concert take place there, and he'd just have one of his black employees go to Memphis and bring the musicians. All seemed, out of nowhere, to have been saved. They had their second chance. Or so they thought.

It was not long after Bradshaw made his offer that there was trouble at the dealership. The trouble had something to do with a black customer suing the dealership for not calling him "Mister," and suddenly the dealership that was going to save them was the center of some very tense racial problems. Bradshaw had to call the boys and tell them that it would no longer be appropriate to have the concert there, given the problems that had developed. The concert was now dead, once and for all, and George and Roger were very angry that they could not pay Will, Charlie, et al back for their kindness and hospitality the previous December.

The last letter that Will sent them was in July of 1962--this one written in yet another hand, and after they'd met John Lee Hooker and arranged to visit Memphis again. His tone has changed, but he seemed not to hold any grudges about the failure of the concert. He even addresses Roger as "Roger," rather than "Mr. Brown," which was his wont:

"Dear Roger

I am very sorry it took me so long to write, but I haven't been able too. I am very glad to hear about John Lee Hooker are you coming too Memphis and you too. I received your clip out of the newspaper + was so glad to get it. Give my love to your family for me.

I am so sorry I couldn't make the trip, because everybody was talking about. Don't give up yet keep on trying. I went got a check-up 7-16-62. I think I have to go back too the hospital. I would write you more but don't has any thing too said I hope you will be down here after you get out of school. Will Shade

P.S. Try to send me a couple of dollar because I am down now."

The mood was, by July, one of subdued desperation. Will's post script may say that he was "down now," but he had already been down. Now he was back to hopeless.

*

One of the musical divisions that segregated Atlantans' experiences was the division between the white audiences for black music, and the black audiences for black music. In Roger and George's high school days, shows were segregated, if not officially, then de facto. When the white kids at Druid Hills High School wanted to hear black music, such as Screamin' Jay Hawkins, The Platters, the Clovers, etc., they would go to the Atlanta Auditorium and the performance was called by them, in good racist fashion, a "jig show." The white kids who went to a "jig show" sat down front apart from the predominantly black audience.

In 1961 or 1962, George and Roger heard that the Staple Singers, a black gospel group whose *Help Me Jesus* LP had excited both of them, were going to be in town. Roebuck Staples, the leader of the group, was a good Delta guitarist--the music was cut from the same cloth as other good downhome Delta music, just as listening to Gary Davis sing spirituals is just about the same as listening to Gary Davis sing blues, except for the lyrics--and George and Roger viewed this as a chance to see some downhome music live. Though neither was religiously inclined, they knew the sound they liked, and this was it.

With great enthusiasm the two approached the ticket window at the Atlanta Auditorium and asked the white guy behind the counter for two tickets. He looked at them very skeptically, and then turned around and went to consult with his supervisor. The "jig show" logic determined that these two should not be here, and he was suffering from a breakdown of audience categories. Roger and George began to worry, suddenly, since the guy was away for some time, but he came back and sold them two tickets. The manager probably figured it would be more potential trouble to keep the two of them out than simply to allow them in and keep an eye on them.

As the two entered the auditorium, the place was packed from top to bottom, and they were faced with a solid sea of black faces. There was not another white face in the place, except for the cops. They took their seats up in the stratosphere and they soon noticed, in one of those odd moments of non-visual perception, that there was someone standing over their shoulders. There was a white cop standing right behind them, assuring that nothing weird or out of place occurred. Though the management and the cops paid them heed, not another soul in the place even acknowledged their existence. There were no problems, no tension, nothing.

When the Staple Singers came out and began to perform, the place just erupted. It exploded. Roger says that he can't remember a similar explosion of energy since. This place was rockin'! People were standing and weaving. They were dancing in the aisles. They were rolling in the aisles. They were shouting and screaming. They were falling down and flopping. They were yelling nonsense and speaking in tongues. People were going into catatonic states and being carried out. And some people went into catatonic states and were passed back over the heads of the crowd. It was amazing, exhilarating music in an atmosphere of excitement unlike anything they'd ever known. When they left the show, it was with a bit of awe for the power of this music in the black community. It remained one of the most exciting musical experiences of Roger's life.

*

In the spring of 1962, after the concert was dead and gone, Roger and George encountered John Lee Hooker. They had heard that Hooker was coming into town, and with the *Country Blues of John Lee Hooker* of 1959 still fresh in their minds, they decided to go see him. They knew that Hooker was going to play at Ponce de Leon Park, the home of the old Atlanta Crackers baseball team, as well as in all of the black clubs, as they knew from WAOK. The Ponce de Leon show was the white show, and the other shows were regarded by them as off-limits then. Roger wonders whether other whites went to the club shows downtown, simply ignoring the old prohibitions; but they assumed, rightly or wrongly, that at these shows they were not wanted. They were determined to see Hooker, however, and they soon found out where he was staying through WAOK.

Hooker was a big name by 1962. He was based in Detroit, but he toured all over the country and in Europe. As big a name as he was, he still stayed in cheap hotels for blacks only. When they arrived at the hotel, Roger and George simply went to the front desk and asked the men there if they could tell them in which room John Lee Hooker was staying. One of the two said: "Dat him tappin' up der now!" And sure enough, they heard a foot beating on the floor. The guys at the desk just gave Roger and George the room number and they went on up. If nothing else, this is a sign of the profound changes that have taken place in American society since 1962.

The two of them made their way upstairs, found the right door, and knocked. Inside, a very intimidating bass voice said "Yeah!" without any tone of hospitality, and they steeled themselves and opened the door. What they saw was rather surprising. Hooker was a little guy with a very deep and intimidating voice. He was sitting on the bed, strumming his guitar, and on an antiquated TV set with a tiny screen, he was watching Tarzan.

Roger and George introduced themselves and they all spoke for a while. Hooker was neither overly friendly nor unfriendly, but he didn't kick them out. They told him they were going to see him at Ponce de Leon Park that night, and they left, thanking him for talking to them. After the show that night, Roger and George flagged him down and invited him to George's home for a fried chicken dinner. He readily accepted, and when George asked him what his drink was, he answered: "Pop." The doctor had taken him off the sauce. They then drove out to the suburbs, where they were greeted by George's mother, who told Hooker it was an honor to have him in their home.

They had a fine dinner, and Roger and George then played him some records and took some pictures on their cheap little camera. They played Hooker the Willie Borum LP that they liked so much. Hooker had never heard of Willie B., but his response was: "He got a good voice!" They also played a Washboard Sam song for him that Hooker liked, particularly the lyric:

I'm too old for the orphans,

Too young for the old folks home.

The evening was a real pleasure for all of them, and no doubt a good diversion for Hooker from the dreariness of touring. Hooker changed hotels, and Roger and George went to his new room to talk some more. He was just sitting in his room between gigs in the middle of the afternoon, and he invited them to come in and sit on his bed while he played. He had a gig, in fact, every night but one that week.

Hooker just sat and played for them all afternoon long. He was playing without electricity, so it began to hurt his fingers, but he still didn't stop. Roger kept asking him to play things he knew from *The*

Country Blues of John Lee Hooker, and Hooker eventually said to him: "Y'all keep askin' for them old numbers!"

Hooker was very modest and unassuming, and his only outburst of bragging was a bit of self-irony: "Can't nobody play like John Lee Hooker!"

Hooker never showed the slightest impatience the whole afternoon. He never looked at his watch, he never sighed. "What a peach of a guy!" Roger says on looking back. "To put up with these two kids for that amount of time..." Hooker just seemed to enjoy their enthusiasm. At some point they asked Hooker if he wanted to play at a party they were going to, expecting him politely to decline, but to their surprise, he agreed. They had even warned him that they could only scrape together $50 from the rest of the people, but still he agreed.

Roger and George returned later to pick him up and drove him out to the suburbs. As they went down the steps to the basement where the party was held, there was spontaneous applause, and Hooker acknowledged the compliment, plugged in his guitar, and began to play. He played for a good couple of hours, including a request from one of the girls present to play his recent hit, "Boom, Boom." When George and Roger thanked him, Hooker kept saying: "I'm payin' my dues to the natural blues." They drove him home later, and that was the last Roger ever saw of John Lee Hooker.

George, however, met Hooker twenty years later in New York. George, who now had a beard, approached Hooker to say hello, and before he could even introduce himself, Hooker said, "That was fun with y'all down in Atlanta." John Lee Hooker is an extremely nice, mellow and unassuming man, and this was what made it so easy for him to entertain a couple of teenagers for hours on end with not a qualm about his own time.

CHAPTER III: ROGER & GEORGE, TENNESSEE, SUMMER 1962

When summer vacation finally arrived in 1962, Roger and George were now high school graduates who would begin at Emory University in Atlanta in the fall. The two of them were extremely anxious to return to Memphis to see Will, Jennie Mae, Charlie, Furry and, they hoped, Gus Cannon, whom they had missed in December 1961. Willie B., with his domineering wife and restrictive contract, was someone they thought it less likely they would encounter.

For this trip, Roger and George brought along a good friend who was also interested in the music, Jim Lester, who brought along his $13 Sears guitar that was missing a string. They also managed to borrow a Norelco reel-to-reel tape recorder from Mark Wilkerson, having learned a hard lesson the first trip. The "Kansas City Blues" that Will and Charlie played for them in their first five minutes of searching on that cold Memphis morning in December was gone, and that wasn't going to happen again. A camera, of course, was also along for the trip this time.

As in December, the three of them loaded into Roger's '57 Chevy in Atlanta and took off across Georgia, northern Alabama, northern Mississippi, and into Memphis. The drive was uneventful, but the weather was definitely the hot and humid Deep South summer to which they were all so accustomed. When they reached Memphis this time, however, the three of them did not make for George's aunt's house, but rather for a cheap hotel. They wanted a bit more freedom of movement this time around, which was harder to gain with a worried aunt waiting up for them. The hotel room was not meant for three people, and Roger recalls that they may have smuggled one of them in to save some money, which was still in short supply.

When the three of them went to Will's place that first morning they were not at all sure how Will and the others would greet them. The failure of the concert, which might have been so important to the lives of these musicians, was still fresh on Roger and George's minds, and they were a bit uneasy at the prospect of confronting them again. With this in mind, the three of them went down to Will's place on

Fourth and Beale and began to climb those same dingy old stairs that lead to his apartment.

As they climbed the stairs they heard an angry voice call out from above: "What're you doin' in my house!" The voice was Will's, but when they looked up, they saw that he was smiling broadly. If they had been worried for about a second, the next second all was well. Will was very glad to see them, and he shook their hands and invited them into his home in his usual hospitable and friendly manner. Jim Lester remembers that Will seemed (perhaps only slightly gleaned by Roger and George at the time) to derive a certain prestige in his community from his role as guide and mentor to these young men; Roger and George probably underestimated the importance of their trips to Will. Their great esteem for Will made it difficult for them to know how unlikely he was to hold a grudge against them for the failure of the concert in Atlanta.

If Will was happy to see them, he was not necessarily happy in the rest of his life. Besides the old poverty and his own poor health, Jennie Mae was in the hospital again, and not at all well. Will worried about her tremendously.

The first day in Memphis they all went to find Gus Cannon, but found that he had moved yet again. Will guided them, eventually, to Gus' new place, and when they found the seventy-nine year-old Cannon he was soused to the gills. They had a tough time in waking Gus up, but even when they had gotten him out of bed he couldn't find his pants. He staggered around in his shorts, and it was only a half hour later that they finally located the pants and left his apartment. Though Gus claimed to them that drinking was what kept him alive, one suspects that he was alive in spite of his constant drunkenness. Booze, Gus used to tell them, was good for his blood. So, with a slowly sobering Gus Cannon in tow, the banjo across his lap, the group of them returned to Will's place and prepared to play. This was easier said than done. Gus, who was already a forty-four year-old veteran of the medicine and minstrel shows for his first recording session (with Blind Blake) in Chicago in 1927, was quite a lot past his prime in 1962. He would probably have been out of practice anyway, and with a good sixty years of dissolute living behind him, it was a miracle that he was still alive.

The upshot of being out of practice was that Gus could not tune his banjo. Will would play a scale on his harp, and Gus would pluck a string in response, but he wasn't succeeding in tuning it. This went on for some time, until Will lost his patience and said: "I can't tune the harp!" After some more attempts, Will said, a bit cruelly: "You've lost your ear!" Gus responded to him, with good old country indignation: "No I ain't!"

Perhaps it should be recalled, at this point, that Will's crowd and Gus' crowd had never played together back in the old days, and Gus was thus not accustomed to playing with Will, Charlie or Furry, who had been playing together, on and off, for forty years. Cannon's Jug Stompers, which featured Noah Lewis on the harp, Elijah Avery, Hosea Woods and Ashley Thompson at various times on guitar or banjo, and Gus on banjo or jug, was centered in the town of Ripley, Tennessee to the north of Memphis, and they were not a part of the Memphis Jug Band scene and vice versa. If there was a bit less friendliness among them towards Gus, this is perhaps a part of it.

The first sessions that were recorded at Will's began with Will and Charlie doing their Memphis Jug Band version of Jim Jackson's "Kansas City Blues" once again, a replay of the tune they performed that first five minutes of the first morning of the last trip. Roger and George felt a bit of the old excitement again on hearing them recreate that important moment of the last trip.

"Eleven Light City," a jumping dance piece, featured Charlie on vocal and tenor guitar, Furry on guitar and Will on his trusty oil can bass. The tune, as preserved on Roger and George's Rounder Records album, starts off a bit ragged, as the musicians try to get together in this informal jam session, but after a few seconds they launch the tune with gusto. Charlie's ebullient vocal and powerful tenor guitar lead the way brilliantly, replete with his trademark "Laughin' Charlie" laugh at the end of a couple of verses:

'Leven light city, sweet ole Kokomo,
'Leven light city, sweet ole Kokomo.
Oh, that 'leven light city,
Baby I know you'll want to go. (heh, heh, heh)
(Instrumental break)
Why did you kiss me? Why did you say good-bye?

Why did you tell me, that great big lie?
'Leven light city, sweet ole Kokomo. (hah, hah)
That 'leven light city, I know you want to go!

Other music from that session includes a version of the 19th century song "Boll Weevil Blues" that Gus, a musician who was seventeen years old in 1900, plays on his banjo, an instrument more of the 19th than the 20th century. The song, as heard on Roger and George's Southland album, is hardly worthy of the man whose "Minglewood Blues" (1928) and "Walk Right In" (1929) are only a couple his masterpieces of jug band musicianship, but Roger recalls that he still had plenty of presence in his old age and remained an extremely friendly and agreeable man.

The next night it was time for Furry Lewis. Furry, who was about seventy at the time, came over in the white overalls that marked him as a sanitation worker for the City of Memphis. He'd been working for the city since 1916. Roger and Jim both recall that Furry was still very formal with them--he was not as quick as Will or Gus to open up to people, and he acted very soberly. Jim Lester recalls that Gus kept calling Furry "Fuzzy," perhaps because there was another neighbor man whom Roger recalls doing so, as well, and it was Jim's Sears-Roebuck guitar, with its missing string, that Furry played that night-- his own guitar was still in hock. Jim recalls thinking that Furry seemed to be the most prosperous of the singers, poor as he may have been.

Also present at this Furry Lewis session, besides the usual roomful of neighbors chatting, laughing and dancing, was the blind amateur musician Abe McNeil, who hung around Will's looking for musical tips. McNeil, who knew Robert Johnson and played some Sonny Boy Williamson (#1) tunes for them, interpolated many a comment into the various tunes, and Will gave him some evil looks a few times when he got out of hand. Being blind, McNeil never got the hint, and kept it up, contentedly, the whole session. His remarks, often quite funny, are a part of the natural blues scene, and they give the session the feel of authenticity that the stilted "Play that thing, boy!", which one often hears on recordings of the 1920s and '30s, lacks completely.

Things got off to a rocky start for Furry when a fuse blew in the apartment, and they had to light candles to go on. There is a wonderful picture of Furry tuning Jim's guitar in the candle light, looking very stately, indeed. But even in a room with only the dimmest light and a cheap guitar less one string, Furry really let loose, a length of brass tubing on his little finger to act as a slide.

For fans of Furry, there is no better example of his rediscovery-era playing, undiminished since his marvelous sessions for Vocalion and Victor in 1927, 1928 and 1929, than on the Rounder and Southland albums. On "Perolee," of which the "Why Don't You Come Home Blues" of his 1927 session is a version, Furry displays both his fine, plaintive vocals and his smooth use of the bottle-neck. His song is complemented, in good back porch fashion, by Abe McNeil:

Perolee, where'd you stay last night?
Perolee, where'd you stay last night?
You didn't come home, till the sun was shinin' bright.
(McNeil: "I wouldn't let 'er go!")
Asked my baby, can she stand to see me cry?
(McNeil: "Say: can she stand to see you die!")
Asked my baby, can she stand to me cry?
Say yeah, Furry, could stand to see you die.
(Bottle-neck weeping on guitar.)
(McNeil: "I like dat verse!")
Could stand to see you die...

The piece was a prime example of blues in its element, and Furry was completely unfazed by Abe's shouted commentary.

Furry also did a couple of beautiful duets with Will, "Muscle Shoal Blues" and "The Train," and a set of solo pieces that appear on the Southland album: "Brownsville Blues," Mistreatin' Woman," which was also in Furry's 1928 session, and "Fare-Thee-Well, Old Tennessee," in which Furry displays well his virtuosity with the bottleneck.

In the next couple of days, before their time was up and their money almost completely gone, there was more recording and more talking. Roger recalls being disturbed that none of the musicians ever seemed to eat--all they did was drink whiskey and wine--and the boys went out to a hamburger stand and bought a bag full of spicy hamburgers for all of them to eat. Will and Jennie Mae, who was now back from the hospital and looking frankly moribund, were very hungry, and the hamburgers were no doubt the most nourishing food they'd had in some time.

It was on the third or fourth day that one morning began with a humorous extempore song by Will, which they called "Wine-Headed Man" on the Southland album, but which could also have been called "Son Brimmer's Golden Harvest Blues."

One of the benefits of having Roger and George visit was that Will had a steady supply of his favorite drink, a cheap, sweet and potent wine called Golden Harvest Sherry. On the day before, there had been no wine, their meager resources being steadily depleted buying booze and food for the musicians, and Will was letting them know that he wanted some today, in humorous fashion. The song is Will's self-reflective parody of the relations between himself and the Atlantans, and is punctuated by the laughter of Roger and George, who had no idea it was coming. The first verse was accidently erased later, but the song went, in full:

Lookahere, Mr. Brown, where'd you stay last night?
Your hair's all rumpled, you ain't treatin' me right!
I'm tired, of your low-down dirty ways!
You wouldn't get me a half-gallon of wine,
Just got me a little ole lousy quart today.
I know when you had your money,
You had friends for miles around.
Money done run out, now none of your friends can be found.
I'm tired, Mr. Brown, of your low-down dirty ways!
You won't give me that half a gallon of wine,
I wish you'd go back to Atlanta and stay.
When you first come up to Memphis,
You were very fine and kind.
Man, you brought me all kinds of wine!
I'm tired, Mr. Brown, of your low-down dirty ways!
You won't buy me enough wine, Mr. Brown,
Just one little ole lousy quart for today.
I woke up this mornin', I was thinkin' good and cool.
I said: "I know Mr. Brown know, Son Brimmer ain't no fool."

He said: "Lookahear, Son, you think you treat me right?"
Said: "I been buyin' you wine, Son, day and night!"
I said: "Lookahere, Mr. Brown, could you tell me one thing?
What's the matter? What you got on your mind?"
He said: "Lookahere, Son Brimmer, I can't buy you wine all the time!"
I said: "Lookahere, Mr. Brown, I don't wanna get mad!
'Cause I'm gonna make you gimme some wine,
Or I'll whip your yas, yas, yas!"
He said: "Lookahere, Son, don't ya get too smart!
'Cause I heard you, when you did that little ole thing last nod."
I said: "Lookahere, Mr. Brown, I don't wanna argue wich you!
Would you give me one of those little ole, good ole, Golden Harvests, too?"
He said: "Well, yes, Son, 'scuse me for bein' so bold.
You know, I'm goin' to buy you one more quart o' wine,
And I gots to bottom it up and go."
I said: "Well, I'm tired, Mr. Brown, of your low-down dirty ways!
Just gimme one more half a gallon,
And I won't bother you no more, today."

The song is both a tribute to Will's ability to compose on his feet and to his sense of humorous irony. It also gives one a look at the relations between the musicians and the high school students through Will's eyes, speaking his most comfortable language: music.

On the last couple of days of music, Roger and George were able to record, among others, Will singing "Beale Street Mess Around," a solo version of the Memphis Jug Band's "Fourth Street Mess Around" (1930) with Abe McNeil adding some vocals and clapping on his bare chest. (The latter effect, of hands on chest, has puzzled many listeners in later years who could not identify the sound properly: was it thigh-slapping? No...) They also recorded Will singing the song "What Must I do?" in which Jennie Mae, over seventy, with one lung and close to death, takes a verse and sings, lustily:

I wonder why I love my long tall man so well?
I wonder why I love my long tall man so well?
Every time he loves me, he makes my belly swell!

As Roger said, she was quite a gal, in the best sense of that word.

An interesting aside on the topic of Jennie Mae's charms had to do with the fact that Furry, upon entering Will and Jennie Mae's apartment, flirted with Jennie Mae rather excessively, patting her cheeks, making lewd comments, and so on. Will did seem too happy about this, but said nothing. It was not long after this trip that Charlie Musselwhite, visiting Will for tips on the harp, wrote to George after witnessing another such visit by Furry that resulted in a drunken wrestling match between Will and Furry on the living room floor. The fight only ended when the two elderly men rolled over, exhausted. Furry, as it happens, had been sweet on Jennie Mae for many a year and Will had always resented it. Even as she neared death, though, she was the apple of seventy-five year-old Furry's eye, and the center of Will's universe.

Another song, this one on the Rounder album, was a duet called "Let Me Ride With You Tonight," featuring Will and a neighbor named Catherine Porter, who contributes a very soulful vocal. The song is really very memorable and puts to shame most of the commercial music one could hear for its combination of soul and style.

The rest of the music, which was jam sessions in an entirely informal setting, was not that memorable. Gus was drunk most of the time, and there are more examples of the ill-effects of whiskey on his playing than are perhaps desirable. When Charlie told Will: "That Banjo Joe can't keep up with us!" it was as much a testament to Gus' deteriorated and drunken state as it was to the lack of sympathy between them.

Abe McNeil was an amateur, not up to the standards even of Gus at eighty and drunk, but he was an interesting man to talk to. He had known Robert Johnson, the obscure figure that he was, and this was exciting to Roger and George. They questioned Abe, but they were later chastised by Mark Wilkerson for their poor interviewing methods: they asked yes-or-no questions, tried to lead the informant, etc. The perfect example of this problem was when they asked Abe the rather foolish question: "Did Robert Johnson like wine, women and song?" To which Abe replied, a bit incredulously: "Why, nacherly he did!"

Another memorable moment was Roger's recollection that the neighbors, some of whom were very skillful dancers, also had their children dancing with them. There was one younger woman, with a daughter about ten years-old, who had the daughter do a lewd dance she called "The Dog." She'd yell: "Do 'The Dog'!" and the little girl would squat down and do a hunching motion with her pelvis, her mother laughing loudly. No one else noticed except to laugh.

*

With their money nearly gone and only fifteen minutes of tape left, the three decided to go back to Atlanta. As they said good-bye to Will, whom Roger would never see again, and who George saw only on his death bed a couple of years later, Will mentioned, off-handedly, that Sleepy John Estes still lived up around Brownsville, Tennessee. This was interesting news to them. Estes' "Special Agent" (1938) had been on the Charters LP in 1959, and it was one of their first loves in blues. Estes' high-pitched, emotional vocals and inventive lyrics were among the best of the blues, and if they could, by some chance, see him--well, it was worth a try, at least. Brownsville was not on the way home, but it was not too far off course, either. They decided, on the spur of the moment, to go up to Brownsville and see if Estes could be found.

They departed on this trip with the same expectations as they had departed on the search for Will in Memphis: he might be dead, and they would most likely not find him. They set off towards Brownsville with high interest and low hopes.

They reached Brownsville, a typical Southern town with a little square in the town center, some stores, and a post office, and they pulled over and asked a black man in his twenties or thirties whether he knew Sleepy John Estes. He responded: "John Adam?" This meant nothing to Roger and George, who didn't know his real name of John Adam Estes, and knew him only from his recordings. When the man repeated: "Yeah--John Adam!" they were still not sure if he knew whom they really meant. The man, at any rate, assured them he knew the person they wanted, and he immediately jumped into the car with them and led them out of town and down a series of winding dirt roads, with an occasional tar-paper shack beside the road.

The car left behind it a trail of dusty clouds, and Roger drove on wondering if they would ever be able to find their way back out. Eventually, however, they reached a particular spot where the man said they would find John Adam. Their guide jumped out and never asked for a ride back, which made Roger wonder how he was going to get back to town. They were on a backcountry dirt road and, still not sure if this was the right place, they got out of the car and looked around.

On the right side of the road there was a tiny shack in very poor condition. On the left side there was a ramshackle house. They asked around and people acknowledged that Estes did, indeed, live there. There were many young children and a few adults in the houses, and Roger and George talked a bit to them. The two young men were astonished at their continued good fortune: they'd found Estes as easily as they'd found Will and Co.

Estes, however, was not home. They waited around a bit, and shortly after their arrival a pickup pulled up in the road and came to a halt. They knew Estes from his pictures and saw him in the front passenger side. He was very thin and looked to be about seventy by now. They half expected him to greet them as jovially as had the outgoing Will Shade and say: "Estes is my name!" or something along those lines. Instead, they approached the pickup and stuck out their hands and nothing happened. There was no reaction because Estes was now blind.

When Estes got out of the pickup they noticed how frail he was. He seemed to be in pretty bad shape and the place around them evidenced real poverty. He immediately sent a little boy off to the tiny shack on the right to fetch his guitar and George got out the tape recorder with its mere fifteen minutes of tape. When the little boy returned, Estes, who was sitting inside the house, immediately began to tune the guitar, speaking little.

Roger and George were not aware that David Blumenthal had been in Brownsville making his movie in 1961, and had already recorded Estes for that occasion. They were also not aware that Bob Koester had already taken Estes up to Chicago to record him for Delmark Records in late March of 1962 while they had been scrambling to save their "Revival of the Blues" concert. As far as they were aware, they were the first blues nuts to find Estes, and they were accordingly thrilled.

Estes had surely not lost his ear, and with a minimum of preparation, plucking the notes up the scale and right out of the tuning of the guitar, he launched into "Rats In My Kitchen" before George even knew what he was doing. They missed a verse, but what they got on tape is splendid Sleepy John:

Oh, I went home last night,
Somewhere 'bout half past ten.
You know they said,
"If you lookin' for groceries, poor John,
You better go and come again!"

The music, which is preserved on the Southland album, is as good as Estes ever performed. His foot--beating out time on the porch floor-- is a perfect accompaniment that gives a good approximation of a bass line, and Estes' vocals were as strong as ever. Perhaps among the most inventive and personal of blues lyricists, Estes gave them his autobiographical "Floating Bridge," also recorded in 1937, "Special Agent," also recorded in 1938, and "Mr. Pat," which he had not previously recorded.

For Roger, this experience was like hearing Will and Charlie play "Kansas City Blues" the previous December. When Estes lit into "Rats In My Kitchen" only a few minutes after their arrival, it was delirium all over again. They could hardly believe they'd found Estes to begin with, and here he was playing his rusty old guitar with (as Jim recalls) a pencil acting as a capo. The experience is one that Roger would never forget.

Roger recalls that after the first song was recorded, Estes had asked a man named Ed, "That was in '38, wasn't it, Ed?" and Ed had answered with a very long, deep, "Yeah" just before the song began. When they played the song back, Ed was extremely amused at the sound of his own voice. Jim Lester recalls that the children all sat around in complete silence, and after they heard the sound of their father's voice on the machine, their faces lit up in joy. They'd never been exposed to tape recording and it was a pleasure to watch their wonder.

Roger also recalls complementing Estes' wife, an attractive woman, younger than her husband and with a scarf on her head in the country manner, on the behavior of her children. There had been not a peep out of them, though there were seven or eight in the area. She smiled, but seemed to understand, as Roger later realized himself, that their behavior was probably dictated by their astonishment that yet more white people were at their house, shaking their father's hand, laughing and chatting with the neighbors, and generally loving their father's music. In the Deep South, out in the sticks, such was hardly a normal state of affairs, but since Blumenthal's visit it was becoming routine.

In addition to the music, George asked Estes a few questions on tape. They asked him about Blind Lemon Jefferson, whom Estes had met, and asked if it were not true that Jefferson was a fat man. Estes responded: "Fine lookin' fella, though!" Another interesting point is that they asked Estes how old he was, and he responded, without hesitation: "Fifty-eight." Not only is it a good way to set his date of birth in 1904, since there has been a certain difference of opinion on this matter, but it was also a surprise to them to see how hard living and poverty could make someone age tremendously. They'd thought he was ten years older than he was.

After the stunning first song, they began to feel the limitations of their fifteen minutes worth of tape. Some regret for burning so much tape of drunken Gus and amateur Abe set in as they realized that they had one of the masters playing for them, and obviously at the top of his form, and they were only going to get a few songs from him. And, indeed, in the middle of a fine rendition of "Mailman Blues," the tape ended, and that was the end of their recording.

With the tape gone and time beginning to press, it was time to leave Sleepy John and go back to Atlanta. When they said they had to leave, Estes asked them for whiskey, but had to settle for the last of their beer and the last four dollars in their wallets. They wished they could pay him better, but this was simply not possible. They started the car and headed for Atlanta and they realized, with some amazement, that they'd only been at Este's place for half an hour at the most. The experience was so intense, the music so good, that they had felt a much longer lapse of time than had occurred. They drove out along the dusty roads, back to the highway, and headed back east to Atlanta without a red cent between them.

 The drive back was a bit harder than the drive there. It was cold on the way back and they had to drive straight through without food or anything to drink. Somewhere in Alabama, when Roger was driving, a cop pulled them over, thinking that there was a drunk at the wheel: Roger was so tired he had been weaving. The cop told them to get some coffee or the result could be the same as being drunk. They made it home without a problem, however, and started at Emory in the fall, as planned.

CHAPTER IV: ROGER & GEORGE, PEG, BIG JOE AND BUDDY IN 1963

In the Fall of 1962, Roger and George were freshmen at Emory University in Atlanta, but George had not stopped his blues activities at all. The fall of their freshman year the two of them were taking part in a fraternity rummage sale in Decatur, selling old clothes to poorer black people. The sale was set up in a vacant lot, and the patrons were blacks who were buying used clothes, not the middle classes, obviously. As they sold the clothes, the ever-alert George asked some of the people what they knew about local blues singers, and he was referred to a couple of guys named Willie Rockomo and Bruce Upshaw.

George went and spoke to Rockomo and Upshaw about singers who might still be around, and, as George commented on my blog in 2012, they gave him the name of another guy "and suggested I ask down at Shorter's Barber Shop." Roger and George, with their friend Jack Boozer, accordingly went down to Decatur Street in the heart of the black section of the city and walked into an old Decatur Street institution, Shorter's Barber Shop.

When they went in to Shorter's, there were a couple of guys being served and a couple more waiting. One guy was having his hair straightened, another just a cut. The boys asked if anyone knew a musician named Peg Leg Howell, and a couple of them, a little guy and a big guy, immediately became animated, saying that they knew who he was. They had a discussion between each other--he's over there on such-and-such a street by so-and-so's house, right?--and they seemed to be thinking of a couple of different people. One of them finally said: "No, no--Peg, you know, *Peg*!" and they seemed to come to an agreement.

The two men led Roger and George over in Roger's car, finally turning down an alley and coming to a shabby one-story house in the thick of the slums. They walked up and knocked on the door, and a thin, faint voice said to come in. They walked in to the dark and dirty house, and there sat Peg Leg Howell on a wheelchair, legless and looking mighty old. They'd been warned that he had no legs, but the general poverty and signs of ill health were over-whelming. They knew him immediately, however, even in his reduced state: he had the same large head that was so impressive in his early pictures. Further evidence was a photograph on the mantle of Peg, Eddie Anthony and Henry Williams standing on an Atlanta street in about 1925. This photo, which has since become quite famous, clinched it in their minds. It must be Peg Leg Howell, who had not recorded since 1930.

Having recorded and met the Memphis people and Sleepy John, Roger and George were accustomed, somewhat, to dealing with much older men and women who had been musically active in the 1920s, but none of the others had been in such bad shape as was Peg. Gus Cannon may have been quite old and an alcoholic, and thus unable to perform to his old standards, but Gus would live past ninety and retain much of his mental sharpness past eighty. With Peg, they encountered a forgotten, legless man whose health was very poor, whose mental state was poor and who was plainly dispirited. An elderly Furry Lewis, still performing brilliantly, was a very different story from an elderly Peg Leg Howell. Peg was an invalid who either sat on his wheelchair or on his bed, and it was obvious that he rarely, if ever, left the house. His only pleasure, they were to discover, was snuff.

Roger, George and Jack entered the house and introduced themselves. Peg's voice was very faint and he was very passive and subdued. They told him that they were interested in his music, and when he saw that they had brought a guitar with them, he reached for it. Peg, who later said that he had given up music in 1934 when his dear friend Eddie Anthony died, began to fumble around with the rustiness of a thirty year hiatus, and he mumbled, faintly, the lyrics:

I wrote you a letter, throwed it in your back yard. (2x)
I would come to see you, but your kid-man got me barred.

They wondered when the last time was that he had sung, but who could guess?

Roger and George arranged to return that evening to see him. They went out with him to another person's house another evening, and they began to see Peg come alive a bit. After many, many years spent as a forgotten invalid living in abject poverty, Peg was showing some pride in himself. In one place he leaned over and said to one of the people present: "You ever heard tell of Peg Leg Howell?" They were happy to see some of the passivity giving way, although plain ill health would not allow all of it to go.

Roger and George went back to see Peg together on a number more weekend evenings. There was a woman, younger than Peg, and either his wife or mistress, who was there when they visited, and she seemed to take care of Peg's needs. Roger remembers very well an illustration of how tough life was over in the black slums in Atlanta. They were over to visit Peg on a Saturday night, and the woman was also there. While they were chatting, the door swung open and a man staggered in holding his back and writhing in pain. He gasped: "They stabbed me with an ice pick!" This was chilling and shocking enough to a couple of white boys from Druid Hills. The response of Peg's woman was, if anything, more shocking to them. She barked out in a sharp tone that would brook no argument: "Don't fall down in here!" The man staggered back out, and Roger guesses that she wanted no police snooping around her place, but the incident was a very scary reminder of the toughness of ghetto life.

After a couple of meetings, they decided to do an album to document Peg's rediscovery. George was able to convince Pete Welding to produce the album for Testament Records, even though it could not be a commercial success. Welding emphasized the documentary significance of the discovery, and went ahead with the project. The thought that Peg could use the money was not far from any of their minds. To prepare Peg to perform, however, was a tough task. He was seventy-five, had diabetes (which is why the other leg was amputated), was exhausted by fighting poverty for so long, and was just plain tired. Years as a shut-in do little for the spirit. George, however, worked with him for a month to help prepare him to perform. Peg's playing was extremely rusty, and he sang so softly that they could not hear him well. His voice regained some of the old force and expressiveness by the time they recorded, but the guitar never really did.

Preparing him to record was a difficult task made worse by the fact that Peg was becoming rather forgetful in his old age. He would forget lyrics to songs, and George had to make posters to hold up in the studio to remind him of the various lines. He also had a tendency to confuse lyrics. Thus, he would sing:

Who been here since I been gone? (x3)
Big black nigger with a derby on.
And then change the lyric to:
Who been here since I been gone? (x3)
Pretty little girl with a derby on.

The second lyric just seemed confused, so he made up a poster for that one, too.

Another difficulty is the rather perplexing problem of Peg's fingernails. For whatever reason, his fingernails were extremely large and thick, and when he played the guitar the nails would clang, loudly, on the body, to the detriment of the music. When George tried to cut the nails, he found that he could not pierce them, and they never could do anything about them. When it came time to record, George taped some foam rubber on the guitar to blunt the clanging.

Worse yet, after a month of preparing, Peg developed a very bad abscessed tooth. His face was badly swollen and the pain was tremendous. When Roger and George offered him aspirin he didn't seem to know what aspirin was and asked them for Juicy Fruit chewing gum. It was a sad session, and Roger remembers the look of compassion on the face of the engineer in the booth when they brought Peg in, inflamed tooth and all.

Another difficulty in the studio had to do with the simple fact that a man with no legs becomes easily unbalanced if he is not holding the arms of his chair. In order to play, Peg had to hold the guitar, and it took some rather fancy balancing and padding from Roger and George to allow Peg to sit up without wavering. The abscessed tooth would have been enough to send the vast majority of people home that day, much less the problem of balance, but Peg was determined and he pulled it off. The result is hardly up to his old standards, but the album documented the rediscovery of a giant of days past and thus was worth doing.

Roger and George were proud of the album. The singing was good, since even a reduced Peg Leg Howell was a good singer, but the playing was not. They were, again, grateful to Pete Welding for taking the financial bath for the sake of the historical moment, and there was also the matter of a check that Welding wrote to Peg, and that George brought to him right away.

Peg was transformed by the experience. He was never one to volunteer his feelings to them, but just the fact that he began to lose his awful passivity and faintness, to assert himself, to ask, with pride, if people knew who they were talking to? This isn't just some invalid, this is Peg Leg Howell! This was a great source of happiness to Roger and George, since they not only loved Peg's old recordings, but liked the man himself, who was very genial with them. He even loaned them his picture with Eddie Anthony and Henry Williams, of which they had a negative made, and which has since appeared in many blues books, thanks to Peg.

In the time that Roger and George spent talking to Peg, they found him a good informant. He gave straight answers without the flourishes and bullshit that often entered the answers of other bluesmen. When they asked Peg about other musicians, he mentioned Georgia Slim and Charley Hicks early on. He didn't seem to know much of anything about the Buddy Moss, Blind Willie McTell and Curley Weaver scene, though.

It had been rumored that Peg had been to New York for a couple of years, and he said, in response, that he'd never been out of Georgia--which Roger believed, saying that Peg was Georgian to the core. When they asked Peg how he'd learned guitar, he just responded: "I learnt myself--didn't take long to learn. I just stayed up one night and learnt myself." When they asked him how he lost his leg, he responded that his brother-in-law shot it off. When they asked him what he did after going to prison for making moonshine whiskey, he said that he went back to making moonshine whiskey. (See the copy of the letter Peg sent the Warden in 1932 that Roger found during later research.) These questions and answers have the believability of an honest simplicity of intention.

Perhaps the most satisfying part of the rediscovery for Roger was the new lease on life they gave to Peg only shortly before his death. Peg had stopped playing music with the death of Eddie Anthony in 1934, as mentioned above, and this says something about the quality of their friendship and about Peg's motivation in playing. He was not seeking celebrity, but was playing as an aspect of his friendship with Anthony. When that friendship died, his music was no longer a central part of his life.

When people say that the Peg album on Testament tarnished Peg's memory because of the substandard performance, this has no effect on Roger for reasons already stated: doing the album was probably the best thing that had happened to Peg in many years; the album documented the rediscovery of an extremely significant and unique musical figure; Peg was able to be paid for the album; and with the presence of a number of songs Peg had not recorded before, it says something more about his repertoire. So, to those who say the album should not have been done, Roger says: "Go fly a kite."

*

George decided to leave Emory for a quarter starting in the Spring of 1963 and take a job at Delmark Records with Bob Koester. Roger, a very serious student, would never have considered such a thing, but George valued the fieldwork and the closeness to the musicians too much to pass up the opportunity to go to Chicago. George managed, in his time at Delmark, to meet most of the big Chicago bluesmen and watch them perform, and along with Mike Bloomfield, to spend quite a lot of time with Big Joe Williams, who lived in the basement of Bob Koester's record store. He met Muddy, Wolf, Sonny Boy, Otis Spann, Little Walter, Little Brother Montgomery, and all the rest in his time on the scene.

In June of 1963, Roger had arranged to go to Montana to punch cattle for the summer--a summer job more adventurous than most! His train, as it happened, would pass through Chicago, and there would be a transfer there, as well. When he told George that he would be passing through, George asked Big Joe if he would play for Roger, to which Joe agreed. Joe, of course, played many informal sets, so it was not too much to ask.

Big Joe Williams was a favorite of both George and Roger's, and it was with great anticipation that Roger awaited the private set in Chicago. Roger also heard some things from George that were interesting. George said that Big Joe was "a perfect gentleman" when he was sober, but when he was drunk he verged on being a dangerous lunatic. Big Joe would become very angry with Koester, and often threatened to kill him when drunk. One time, as George recalls, Big Joe was drunk and angry, and he began to threaten George, but saying, all the while, "I'm gonna beat the shit out of you, Bob!" George kept trying to deflect the anger by saying that he wasn't Bob, but this did no good, and George actually feared for his life. Life with Big Joe was a mixed blessing for all concerned, but it seemed to be worthwhile to all of them to risk his drunken irrationality.

When Roger arrived in Chicago George was there to pick him up at the station and transport him to Koester's shop at 7 West Grand. George introduced Roger to Koester and Big Joe when they arrived, and then they all went down to Big Joe's basement apartment. There was some joking among the three that Roger had not understood at the time: Joe kept saying something about "Piney Woods" or something along those lines, and Koester was laughing--the album that George and Roger had loved so much was Delmar 602, *Piney Woods Blues*, released in 1960, and it was from this album that Joe would play.

Big Joe was very impressive, physically. He was short and stocky, wore a white shirt and a hat, and had very muscular arms and loose wrists, all the better to flail the 9 string guitar with. When they got down to the basement, Big Joe reached for his beat-up old guitar and "started whippin' with those fat, stubby fingers of his." He reeled-off half a dozen numbers from his first Delmar album, including "Peach Orchard Mama" (also recorded for Blue Bird in 1941), "Baby Please Don't Go" (also 1935), and "Tailor-Made Babe." Roger sat at his feet, transfixed by the power of the performance and the mastery of the guitar and vocal.

To Roger, this was seventh heaven. It ranked, musically, with Will and Charlie's rendition of "Kansas City Blues" in Memphis in December, 1961, and with the performance of "Rats in My Kitchen" by Sleepy John in 1962. The primary difference, and what made it less of a gut-wrenching experience over-all, was that he was expecting to hear Big Joe, had done nothing to discover him, and that Big Joe was all set up and ready to go when he arrived. The experience was an aesthetic high of great proportions, however.

When Big Joe finished has last number, Roger was convinced that he was going to miss his train. He jumped up, thanked Big Joe and Koester, and ran out to a cab, still reeling from the headiness of the experience. He told the cabby to step on it and just made it to his train. But to hear Big Joe in so personal and informal a manner it was more than worth it.

*

In the same year that Roger heard Big Joe in Chicago, George Mitchell set out to Atlanta to make contact with Buddy Moss (1914-1984), who had recorded some sides in the 1930s and '40s with Curley Weaver, Josh White, Fred McMullen and the Georgia Cotton Pickers (Weaver, Barbecue Bob and a teenaged Moss). Neither George nor Roger knew Moss's music, but George said in 2012 that "I had heard of Buddy Moss, and that he could still be alive, from one of Koester's 78 auction lists I got through the mail," so he set out hoping to find Buddy by going back to some people he knew from their time with Peg Leg Howell.

"The person who told me about Buddy Moss," says George, "was the owner of the house where we took Peg to record him because Peg had no electricity. The name Albert Yarborough comes to mind...Albert told me where he [Buddy] lived, and I went to his apartment the next evening." Contrary to what I had said in the first edition of this book, George said that Bob "Koester did not send me to Atlanta about Buddy; Koester never sent me anywhere."

Having learned where Buddy Moss lived, George went to Buddy's house on Park street and introduced himself. George's plan was that there would be trial recordings made at George's house on Woodview Drive, and that these recordings would be sent to Bob Koester in Chicago to decide on the possibility of doing a Delmark album. Buddy had not recorded since 1941, so it would be a re-entry into the music world for him, though he had continued to play in the intervening years and was better than ever in 1963.

The session was, in fact, a brilliant one. Buddy's guitar work had been good in the 1930s and 40s, and now it was virtuoso level. The set included his song "Mamie," which was covered by Blind Boy Fuller in 1937, "Hey Lawdy Mama," and a version of Leroy Carr's "In the Evening." There were short takes of "1000 Woman Blues," "Some Cold Rainy Day," and "Unfinished Business" in addition to the regular length songs. Buddy was in top form and Koester was very impressed once he heard the demos.

Anyone at all familiar with Moss knew that he was a rather difficult man, to put it mildly. Though it was not a good idea to mention it in public if one wished to remain on Buddy's good side, there was a hiatus in his recording from 1935 to 1941 that was always left mysteriously blank in his own telling of his biography. It was blank, of course, because Buddy was in prison serving a life sentence for the murder of his common-law wife, Roberta Ward. He'd been released after seven years on condition that he leave Georgia for good. Buddy's famous temper was placed side by side with terrible jealousy, and the combination was awful.

Willie Mae Jackson, Barbecue Bob and Charley Lincoln's sister, told Roger that Roberta had gone to a store, then to her mother's house to see a visiting sister, and came running home. Buddy met her at the door and asked her where she'd been. She snapped: "To the store." Buddy was obviously insinuating that she'd been with another man. They exchanged a few words and, as Piano Red told Roger, "Buddy started shooting that young girl like a rabbit." Ernest Scott said that he shot her three times, and the death certificate says that it was a shot through the heart that killed her.

Piano Red said that Buddy played for the guards while in prison, and this sometimes gained him a reprieve from the chain gain. When he was released, it was to work on a farm in North Carolina, where he drove a truck and worked hard. Red also said: "He didn't agree with nobody--he had the wrong attitude. Curley got along with him. They let him have his way [because he was such a good musician], and that made him worser and worser." Ernest Scott, in understated fashion, said of Buddy: "He's got funny ways."

Well, none of this could be stated in public or Buddy would never speak to you again. Two blues researchers, in fact, found this to their discomfiture in the early '70s. They had visited Buddy many times and had written something that included a reference to his time in jail, which Buddy got wind of. The next time they went to pay Buddy an informal visit, just to say hello, Buddy took them to task for their error, and proceeded to chase them from his house with a pistol. He was very sensitive about his reputation, and wanted nothing of his murder to be known in public.

Dealing with so difficult, even irrational, a man is always a chore. His great talent made him a very desirable man to know, but it was very tough not to wind up on his shit-list or simply to be disappointed by his behavior. The Delmark album, for instance, which would have placed Buddy back on the musical map, never was recorded. The trial recordings, recently released as a CD and with Roger's liner notes, are all that came of the contact with Koester, since Buddy made unreasonable demands (see above) and refused to budge.

Paranoid about being ripped-off, Buddy could also kill himself by his suspicions. In fact, John Hammond, Sr. later brought Buddy to Nashville to record some songs for album release--this time Buddy gave his blessing to the project, but the album never appeared. This, of course, led Buddy to believe that they wanted the songs, but were willing to wait until he died to release them so they would not have to pay him. The songs, by the way, are set to be released by Sony, though one suspects that the delay in bringing them out was not for the reason Buddy believed. His irrationality was hardly an asset.

Other than his Biograph LP of 1966 and some festival appearances, Buddy never made it in his potential second career, partly because he was so difficult, partly because he was unwilling to compromise, as Josh White, for instance, was. Roger heard from Fred Ramsey that Buddy performed brilliantly at the Newport festival, and that the audience didn't like him. He knew this was the case, and when he said so to Ramsey backstage, Ramsey said that it was true that they hadn't liked him, but that he'd been damn good. The folknik audience, waiting for Bob Dylan (or some other folk-pop hero), was unable to appreciate the artistry of Moss, but he refused to play "folk music" to satisfy their demands.

Buddy's non-career may have been different had a 1964 meeting with another bluesman (of sorts) been more influential upon him. It was in 1964 that Josh White came to Emory for a concert, and George and Roger went to the show. Roger never tires or railing against White, and he says that the show was "nauseating." George brought Buddy along, and they went up to White after the show to say hello. Buddy and White had recorded some sides together in New York in 1935, but they had not kept in touch since then, so it seemed that he was happy to see White all those years later.

George and Buddy went up to White after the show, and White told them that he was going to a party in town, and they should come along. They agreed, and Buddy and White stayed up all night talking, drinking and playing. They reminisced and chatted at great length, and White kept pushing Buddy to get his career back on track. For those curious to know if Buddy commented on White's musical style, George never heard it if he did: he fell asleep long before the two older men were ready to call it a night. It is even possible that Buddy took White seriously at first about his career: he managed to be cooperative enough to put out a fine LP of live material on Biograph in 1966, even if he'd shot down the Delmark album a couple of years before.

As Roger always says of Buddy, he was a born loser--the guy who always found a way not to succeed. What this meant to Buddy was that he was always equally bitter, suspicious and angry with all of the people who were trying either to help him or exploit him. George Mitchell, who was always trying to help Buddy to get his career going, wound up on Buddy's shit-list because, as he later told Roger (who had to spend a good bit of time listening to Buddy drag George over the coals and bite back any response): "He's got no right to use my name!"

As George says, "Buddy was definitely enraged about my using his name in an interview with Charters, who quoted me about where he was born, stuff like that. However, by the time I had moved back to Atlanta, Buddy seemed to have forgotten that as far as I could tell, and we never had any problems that I can remember. I spent some time with him here and there, and for this and that, before starting to run festivals for which I hired him."

Roger managed to stay on Buddy's good side by being very careful. He always brought Buddy a bottle of Bourbon when he visited, and was very careful to tip him properly when he played for him as a favor. He would send a Christmas card with a ten or twenty dollar bill enclosed as a token of appreciation. Though Buddy was not as poor as Peg had been, Buddy's non-career meant that he and his wife, Dotty, were not living much above poverty, and were dependent on their crumby day jobs to get by.

Roger almost always found Buddy very accommodating when he visited. He remembers the many times he would drop in to visit, and he'd ask Buddy, apologetically, if the ax was around--he knew how many people were bugging Buddy for his time. But Buddy never begrudged him a single session. He would always respond to Roger's apologetic attitude with the generous insistence that he needed the practice. Buddy could become touchy, however, if there was a recorder around. Roger got Buddy to record "Hey Lawdy Mama" in 1971 at his father's house in Decatur, and when he asked, in his enthusiasm, for "1000 Woman Blues," Buddy just shook his head and said, "I done give you that." Roger knew Buddy well enough simply to back off and leave the matter at that.

Buddy was not too proud to admit that he had influences, odd as it may seem in so head-strong a man. Roger recalls Buddy sitting down one night and running through a series of riffs. He'd say: that one was Lonnie Johnson; that was T-Bone Walker; that was Blind Blake. His real inspiration, however, was Gary Davis, the blind preacher from South Carolina whose beautiful, whimsical, and intricate guitar playing was the epitome of the Piedmont style. Towards Blind Boy Fuller, who many assume was Buddy's mentor in music because they sound alike, Buddy was not so generous. Fuller's popularity was actually something that had come about after Buddy went to prison, and Fuller's fine playing and singing were influenced by the incarcerated Buddy, not the other way around. Buddy scoffed at the idea that he was imitating Fuller, whom he'd never met, and once said to Roger: "Blind Boy Fuller couldn't play no guitar!" He acknowledged the influence of the masters, such as Blake and Lonnie Johnson, but would never accept the idea that Fuller was anything but a student of his own records of the 1930s.

As the 70s went on and Buddy's shit-list grew, his activities declined to almost nothing and his temper and behavior never improved. Roger worked hard to get him a couple of gigs in the early 70s, and Buddy backed out at the last minute for patently flakey reasons. As his health declined with old age and hard living, Buddy's playing degenerated and he really couldn't perform well enough by the later 70s to do more than an occasional festival, such as the roots festival organized by George in Atlanta in 1979.

One of Buddy's interesting traits was that he would play all night if there were young women around: if George and Roger went to a party where Buddy was playing, he was always more out-going and energized if there were lots of girls in the room. Roger recalls this fondly because he brought his young wife with him in about 1969 to listen to Buddy, and Buddy just would not stop playing. Roger found a forgotten piece that he'd recorded in the later 60s at Buddy's in the last couple of years, and dated it by the fact that he and his wife exclaimed their approval at the end. When Buddy wanted to impress the ladies, there were no limits.

Perhaps Buddy's irritatingly complex and manic behavior were a combination of (what surely sounds like) manic depression and harsh living. He was a fantastic musician and a very poor organizer of careers. His anger was simply too much out of control for him to be trustworthy. His career, such as it was, can be summed up best in something he said to Roger on many occasions, and in particular with reference to Hammond and the Nashville scenario: "I may be poor-- but I'm not gonna be poor so you can be rich!" He was proud, angry and often irrational, but he got a lot of leeway because of his brilliance as a musician. As Piano Red said, this indulgence only made him worse.

CHAPTER V: ROGER AND GEORGE, LATE 60S, NEW ORLEANS, ATLANTA, L.A.

In the later 1960s to 1973, Roger did his graduate work in German at the University of Kansas, in Lawrence. As it happened, Memphis was midway between Atlanta and Lawrence and Roger stopped in to see Furry and Gus whenever he made the trip. Charlie and Will had died in 1965 and 1966, very soon after each other, and though Will was always ill and Charlie seemed perfectly healthy, it was Charlie who died first. When Roger managed to locate Robert Burse, Charlie's down-and-out brother (who had played drums on a few of the Memphis Jug Band's later sides) and ask him how Charlie had died, he said: "He just took sick an' died!"

Roger saw Gus on each visit, but his ability to play was decreasing ever more rapidly. He had stopped drinking whiskey by this time (which was a bad sign for Gus, since he thought that it was whiskey that kept him alive!), and only drank beer. His arthritis was bad and he said of it: "It's a mess!" Gus had a new wife by this point, and there was an extremely vicious dog that Gus was only able to restrain from attacking Roger by holding it back with his cane. When Roger returned again on the next trip, the dog was in a cage. Gus told him that he'd bitten a couple of people and "We done put him in jail!"

Roger would always ask Gus lots of questions, and for a man born in 1883 he had a fine memory that went way back. Gus was particularly good on personnel and he could tell you when Alan Shaw was playing, or when it was his son, etc. Bengt Olsson, who published a book called *Memphis Blues* in 1970 (from which the acknowledgements were eliminated, thus deleting his thanks to Roger for photographs and information), was always feeding Roger with questions, as was Roger's German friend Karl Gert zur Heide, whose *Deep South Piano* was also published in 1970. Gus loaned Roger a picture of himself in blackface for a minstrel show in the teens or twenties, which Roger then loaned to Olsson, and so on.

Gus was not the only person to whom Roger would speak on behalf of Karl Gert or Bengt. Roger spoke to the Memphis old-timer

Dewey Corley, who told him that he had taught Roosevelt Sykes how to play piano way back when.

*

In 1972 or 1973, Roger happened to be in Atlanta at the same time as the researcher Pete Lowry, with whom he was acquainted. Lowry offered to show Roger some of the finds of his research, a number of older guys who'd been a part of the Atlanta blues scene, but had never recorded. These were men such as Charlie Rambo, Ernest Scott, Jonas Brown, Emmit Gates and Buddy Keith.

The most exciting musical find of them was Charlie Rambo, who was about seventy, but still very musically sharp. Rambo had a very fine homemade eight-string guitar, a piece of folk art that was universally admired. Rambo had placed silver dollars in the body of the guitar, as well as other assorted decorations, and he was a very deft musician. Roger and Pete found Rambo where one always found him: on his back porch. Rambo was a very diffident, friendly, man whose cordiality was completely unaffected. They approached him, Pete introduced Roger to him, and he immediately offered to play.

Rambo had been an associate of Blind Willie McTell's in the old days, and to hear him play was a remarkable thing. Roger said: "When he played, you thought you were hearing Willie McTell!" The problem with Rambo is that he was too shy to sing. He would play his guitar, in which he took an enormous amount of pride, but he had too little ego to sing along with it.

As they sat on Rambo's back porch in the black ghetto of Atlanta, an older black man came along to say hello. When he arrived, they'd been talking about making the guitar talk, a McTell trademark (e.g., "Travelin' Blues" (1927)), and the guy told them a story that he said was true, but he had tongue firmly in cheek. He said that there was a musician who could make his guitar talk, and he had a run-in with a cop. He was angry at the cop, and when the cop turned and walked away, he made his guitar say: "Son of a bitch!" The cop heard what the guitar said and went right back and arrested him. They all laughed.

It was this sort of event--good country blues punctuated with a mellow tale told by a genial neighbor--that characterized the time one spent with Charlie Rambo. This was the last time Roger heard him play, since Rambo had a stroke not long after, and he could no longer perform. He remained every bit as genial, however, and when he and George went back to see him a few years later, they enjoyed his company enormously.

Roger and Pete also went to see Ernest Scott, a Buddy Moss protégé. They found him and listened to him play, and then they talked to him for a while. They asked him about Buddy, and Scott said that he had always loved Buddy's playing, but could not understand the man himself. How he could shoot his wife down so heartlessly out of the merest jealous doubts was beyond Scott, and he just shook his head. Like all the other informants to whom one spoke about Buddy, he seemed to think that Buddy's temper was something that gave him too much power over other people, since people were prone to let him have his way. When they asked Scott if he'd done any traveling, he said he'd spent some time in New York City. When they asked why he went, he gave a good bluesman's answer: "Just gwine!"

*

In 1973 Roger received a summer research grant from Hiram College in Hiram, Ohio, where he'd begun to teach that year, to go to Los Angeles and visit the John Edwards Memorial Foundation (JEMF) at UCLA. The JEMF was a real gold mine for blues enthusiasts: Edwards had been a prof interested in linguistics, and he'd conceived the idea of using "race records" to study black American dialects. Edwards had bought 78s by all of the blues artists and preachers he could lay his hands on, he'd played them only a couple of times to get the idea of the dialect, and then he'd put them into an archive. So, while many blues reissues are only available from a disc that languished for many, many years in the closet of a Mississippi shack, these recordings were pure and in perfect shape. When Fullerton received this collection it was a real find for blues researchers.

Roger went to JEMF in the summer and spent as much time as he could in listening to records by people whom he'd been unable to find before. Music professor David Evans, who worked at Fullerton and was affiliated with the JEMF, was a good contact, and he and Roger had a long conversation that summer. When Roger said that he was from Atlanta and detailed his various blues adventures, including rediscovering Peg, Evans suggested that Roger might be interested in talking to the man who started much of the recording of hillbilly and "race" artists in Atlanta: Polk C. Brockman. Brockman was still alive and in retirement in Florida and this seemed like a good idea.

Brockman was born in 1899 and worked in his father's furniture business, which, in 1923, also sold phonographs and records, and this department it was Brockman's job to manage. Brockman's industry was such that the department soon became more profitable than the rest of the store and became the largest retail outlet for Okeh records, the Ralph Peer company that had pioneered "race" recording with Mamie Smith's "Crazy Blues" in 1920. There were even branches of Brockman's retail business in Richmond, Cincinnati, New Orleans, Memphis and Dallas.

Brockman had pushed the distribution aspect, but this was not his great contribution to the recording industry (and thus to blues enthusiasts, who would have no record of the blues sung earlier in the century besides elderly musicians). Brockman began the push to tap the hillbilly and "race" markets by finding original artists and putting their music on wax. While most of the record market in 1923 was concentrated in classical and parlor music for white audiences, and the blues craze was dying down during a period of economic trouble, Brockman decided that some of the hillbilly artists he'd seen (quite incidentally--he had no interest in hillbilly or black music himself) would sell to an audience that had not been courted as yet, particularly the hillbillies who'd come to live in Atlanta and work in the mills. It was Fiddlin' John Carson, an old-time country musician, who was his biggest find, but there were others of them in the aftermath of the enthusiastic response to the music. Brockman's boss, Ralph Peer, who had doubted the advisability of putting this material into the stores, was quite sold on the idea when the money started pouring in.

Brockman also later tapped the "race" market in Atlanta, and this was what interested Roger. With Evan's tip in mind, Roger went to the office of an old Atlanta friend who was living near Los Angeles, in Manhattan Beach, and who had a national WATS Line, and made his call to the Brockman residence. When he called, Roger first spoke to Brockman's wife. She was a very genial person, and it was in his discussion with her that Roger learned something both interesting and irritating. When Mrs. Brockman asked Roger where he'd lived in Atlanta, Roger responded that it was North Decatur Road. When she asked the number, with curiosity in her voice, he said 1568. Mrs. Brockman said: "That's between Springdale and Briarcliff!" Roger said that it was, and she said: "We lived between Springdale and Oxford!" All those years as a budding blues enthusiast and Roger had lived exactly one block from the Brockmans. He could have walked down the street and picked his mind when Brockman had been a younger man, but it was not to be.

When Roger then spoke to Brockman, he found out how he'd found artists to record in the 1920s and into the 1930s. He made a regular weekly visit to the "81" Theater on the very busy Decatur Street, where he discovered and recorded the comedy team Butterbeans and Susie and the pianist Eddie Heywood. He would also wander about and approach street musicians and musicians at dances. He also made a point of finding preachers to record, and it was the prolific Rev. J. M. Gates who was his biggest find. He also traveled to various other sites in search of talent, and he recorded Blind Lemon Jefferson, in spite of the latter's Paramount contract, and the Mississippi Sheiks (Bo Carter, et al) as a result of these travels.

When Roger asked him to reminisce about the black artists he'd known, Brockman was pretty blank. He'd never liked either hillbilly music or blues, had kept no memorabilia, and had commented in an article in the *Orlando Sentinel* that if he were going to buy records, he preferred "fine classical music." The "if" in the previous sentence suggests that he didn't buy even classical, and as his wife said, affectionately, of his taste in music: "He liked the sound of the cash register." Roger asked Brockman about Sloppy Henry and some of the other more obscure figures and there were no memories at all. Brockman readily volunteered information about Daisy Douglas, of whom Roger had never heard, and said he had quite liked her. Roger was able to find a recording of Daisy Douglas's at the JEMF, and he said it was the most beautiful "St. Louis Blues" he'd ever heard. He also suspects that the fiddler on the song was Eddie Anthony.

When Brockman told Roger that he'd recorded Blind Lemon in Atlanta (in March 1927, according to Godrich and Dixon), Roger was amazed. (Roger later sent Brockman the only picture that we have of Jefferson, and Brockman said it was a good picture of him, all right.) Brockman had run into Lemon in Dallas and had arranged for him to come record in Atlanta. No one seemed to be overly concerned with Jefferson's Paramount contract. When Roger asked if there was any hesitation on Lemon's part to violate the other contract, the phlegmatic Brockman just chuckled and said: "No, he was ready."

Brockman, as it happened, went back to Atlanta on one train and Lemon followed, later, on another one. When Lemon didn't show for some time after he was supposed to be there, Brockman was worried about him--a blind man on a long train ride could get lost or in trouble in many ways. As it turned out, Lemon showed up later and explained to Brockman that he had gotten off the train in Shreveport, since he'd never seen the town! Brockman told Roger: "He got around remarkably well for a blind man." They did some sessions for OKeh, but because of later problems of contract violation, only two of seven tunes, "Black Snake Moan" and "Matchbox Blues," were issued.

Brockman recalls another incident concerning Blind Lemon. In light of the incident in which Lemon got off the train in Shreveport just to get a look around, Brockman suspected that Lemon could take care of himself just fine. He got proof one day when Lemon asked a man named Tom Rockwell for $5, and the man gave him a $1 bill to see what would happen. Brockman recalls that Lemon simply retorted: "That ain't no $5 bill!" Maybe Lemon knew when people were playing games with him from the tone in their voices, or maybe it was an old gag to play on blind people that he could see coming a mile away.

The last musicians of whom Brockman had any real memories were the Mississippi Sheiks, whom he had discovered, quite by accident, in Shreveport, Louisiana. After the success of their songs such as "Stop and Listen Blues," Brockman picked them up in Jackson and drove them all the way to San Antonio for a recording session. Godrich and Dixon list San Antonio sessions for the Mississippi Sheiks in June, 1930 and March, 1934, and it was in 1930 that Brockman drove them down. He didn't remember anything about the music, but he remembered the men themselves. "They were good boys; they were all right."

Perhaps the Brockman figure whose sides were most prolifically pressed were those of Rev. J. M. Gates, the most popular preacher of his day. From his first OKeh session in 1926 to his last OKeh sessions in 1930 (Godrich and Dixon say that he continued to record for Bluebird till 1941), Gates recorded many sides for Brockman, along with his "congregation" of Sister Norman, Sister Bell and Deacon Leon Davis. Brockman told Roger that the public figure of the Rev. Gates was a put-on: he was a very quiet and gentle man in private, and the fire and brimstone that he hurled so well in the pulpit was for the good of his congregation's souls, not an indication of what he was like, himself. Brockman also recalled having to bail the good Deacon Davis out of jail on a good number of occasions to record Gates. Davis was a regular in the drunk tank, and Roger asked "Was he really a deacon?"--Brockman just smiled, and said: "In those days, any black man who went to church was called a deacon!"

It was Gates, in fact, who recorded a couple of pieces that the market-savvy Brockman suggested, and Gates performed off the cuff. One of the songs is the surreally entitled "Death May Be Your Santa Claus," and the other is the rather obvious device called "Pay Your Furniture Man." The latter 78 was given away by furniture store owners in Atlanta.

Brockman told Roger that his method of working with artists was set. He paid a flat fee, no royalties, and the first couple of tunes they recorded were done for free, "Sort of a test deal," to see if they were acceptable. Brockman said that he had never been refused by anyone he had approached to record for him. Finally, drinking was discouraged in the studio, but Brockman figured that a little nip at the bottle couldn't hurt anyone if it relaxed the performer a little. As he said, if the guy wanted a nip, "Let him go."

Brockman made a killing on record companies until the early 1930s when the Depression killed the market for blues and hillbilly music--poor people can be targeted as a market only in a strong economic atmosphere, after all. In 1932, Brockman bought Columbia's entire "race" and hillbilly catalog for two cents apiece, later selling them for ten cents. Then in 1934, Brockman bought the distributorship for Columbia in Georgia, Florida, and North and South Carolina for only $1600, and this really put him in the money. After a trip around the world, Brockman got out of the record business entirely in 1938 and went back to a profitable wholesale business in musical instruments and supplies. He later retired in Winter Park, Florida and lived out a contented retirement there with his wife. This is when Roger caught him and the only regret Roger has is that he and George had not gotten to him earlier.

*

In 1971, Roger had taken the Ph.D. in German from The University of Kansas and landed his first teaching job at Hiram College. He had not been in Hiram long before he discovered a colleague, a professor of music named John Burley, who was interested in New Orleans jazz. When Roger learned that Hiram had a system, then, of three quarters and a three week "Interterm" during which one hour courses were offered between Fall and Winter quarters, he and Burley decided that they would do an Interterm course on jazz and blues in New Orleans.

It was an odd coincidence, as Roger planned the New Orleans trip, that he discovered that the son of the famous jazz and blues scholar Fred Ramsey was a student at Hiram, and the son also found out about Roger. Fred Ramsey got in touch with Roger and offered some tips and ideas for the trip, since he'd done a good amount of Louisiana field work, and told him about a find of his--an old country blues singer and guitarist named Scott Dunbar in Lake Mary, Mississippi. Roger thanked Ramsey, and put Dunbar on the agenda.

The arrival of the group in New Orleans began with an encounter with some good Deep South racism. When they arrived at the hotel, the woman who ran it noticed that there was a black girl among the students. She told Roger and Burley, foreboding of disaster in her voice, that the girls were all going to have to share a bathroom, and Roger, who was from Atlanta and accustomed to these sorts of people, simply said that this would be fine, and the girls didn't mind. Burley, however, was from Smith Center, Kansas and he had really never met with this brand of racist. He was very surprised. When the woman began to go on about how the country was going to hell because of the policies of the government, Roger knew what was coming but Burley didn't. The woman's favorite phrase was: "This house wasn't built on that!" and she meant by this liberal attitudes in general, anti-racism in particular.

At some point in the discussion, Roger knew that things were coming to a head because the woman began to vituperate against a black alderman in New Orleans who was trying to change the way the city was run, and the woman began to become even more animated. She seemed to steel herself, and finally blurted out: "We're not gonna let the niggers take over! This house wasn't built on that!" Burley's jaw, Roger remembers, dropped in almost comic book fashion. He was utterly amazed. Roger just wanted to change the topic and managed to come up with: "When was your house built?" which sent her off on her ancestors, thankfully.

The study trip involved listening to jazz and blues artists live and on record and listening to lectures. They were scheduled to look for Babe Stovall, Snooks Eaglin and a few others of the most famous artists still around and available. Dunbar was an alternative to Eaglin, for those who wanted to go. Dick Allen of the Tulane University Archives of Jazz was Roger's most important local contact, and Allen helped them find a few of the artists, since they trusted him implicitly. No one, as Roger put it, ever mistook Allen for a bill collector or cop, which was often the case with others. It was at the Archive, in fact, that Roger met James Larocca. After they'd become friendly, Larocca told Roger that he and his girlfriend were going down to the country to see the bluesman Robert Pete Williams and asked if he'd like to go. Roger, of course, accepted, passing on Snooks Eaglin.

Roger knew of Robert Pete from his festival performances and from some of his recordings, but it was not a music he knew much about. Robert Pete's music is definitely sui generis: it is rambling poetry set to guitar, with little melody, and little in the way of beginnings, middles and ends. He tended to pick up the guitar and play, but he was not the bluesman who would say: "Now I'll play such and such a song." It was more of a poetic stream of consciousness with guitar accompaniment. If Roger could go to Buddy Moss and ask him to play "Mamie" or "1000 Woman Blues," there was no similar thing he could do with Robert Pete since he couldn't distinguish one song from the other on the little listening he'd done.

When Roger and the others arrived at Robert Pete's shack way out in the country, they saw a truck out front with scrap metal heaped in back. Roger assumed that Robert Pete collected scrap metal for a living, or at least for part of it. One of the things that really interested Roger in Robert Pete was this rustic quality--he was very down-home. David Evans had told Roger that Robert Pete was a very warm guy and it was the truth. Robert Pete greeted them with great kindness and brought them into his home with all the courtesy that they could ask.

Robert Pete was a sweet, unassuming guy, and it was hard to picture him as a murderer. He was, of course, first recorded in the state pen, where he was serving a life sentence for murder, and this picture was nearly impossible to reconcile with the kind man who greeted them. Roger discovered that Robert Pete kept a pistol in his glove compartment, which convicted felons aren't supposed to do, since he lived in the heart of Klan country and he wanted to be able to defend himself from the Klansmen if the need arose.

So, Robert Pete had them in and just played and played his free form blues poetry and there was no drinking at all. While Pete Guralnick said that Robert Pete drank a whole bottle of whiskey while they were with him for an afternoon, Roger said there was no drinking when he visited--he was sorry to see that Robert Pete smoked, though, since he had a heart condition. The performance was a bit hypnotic, and watching Robert Pete's fingers at work on the guitar was very impressive. All told, Roger says he prefers a song with beginning, middle and end, but that watching Robert Pete was fantastic.

Robert Pete was apparently very superstitious. He wanted to read tea leaves in one person's cup and he was quite anxious to share his beliefs with Roger and his other guests. Being completely illiterate and unschooled he was truly inside "folk" culture, and this was also very interesting to see. (He told Roger proudly that, though he was illiterate, he could sign his name and he "could count pretty high"!)

The only dreadful thing that happened on the visit to Robert Pete was an incident that Roger still recalls incredulously. At one point the next day, Robert Pete's teenage son came up to Roger and said he wanted to talk to him. He took Roger aside and said: "Hey man--you know Johnny Cash?" Roger was dumbfounded at first and unable to respond. He could barely believe it. "To me, Johnny Cash is tone deaf!

This guy's the son of a musical genius and poet, and he's a Johnny Cash freak..."

That night the three visitors slept comfortably in a house that could not have been big enough for this to be the case--there must have been some kids sleeping in the barn! They arose the next morning to be greeted by a concerned Robert Pete: "You rest good?" They had a good breakfast and left Robert Pete's with a very high opinion of both his music and his hospitality.

*

Later in the New Orleans trip Roger finally decided to find Scott Dunbar. Fred Ramsey had said that Dunbar was a very fine country blues musician, though probably about seventy, and that his wife was a very sharp lady and fine Creole cook. Roger discovered from Ramsey that it was necessary, in order to locate Dunbar, to leave a phone message at the general store in Lake Mary and they would relay the message when he came in from the country. Roger called from Dick Allen's office and a few days later Dunbar called back. Roger will never forget Dick Allen calling him to the phone at the Archives, picking up the receiver, and hearing a slow, mellow, deep voice drawl on the other end: "Who you is?" This was Scott Dunbar: uncomplicated back-country.

Having arranged a time to meet him, Roger went to see Dunbar along with a few Hiram students and Dick Allen. Dunbar just hooked up his amp and said: "You be able to hear this for a mile!" (to which Allen muttered, aside, to Roger: "That's what we're afraid of!"). Dunbar played for about an hour. His style was neither Delta nor any other particular style, Roger says--just Scott Dunbar. He poured out his versions of "Sweet Mama Rolling Stone" and "Baby, Please Don't Go," among others. He was a rocking guitarist though their fears about volume were proved unjustified.

Dunbar, as an informant, was rather limited. His wife would have served much better but she was not along. Dunbar had a tendency to exclaim, after playing a song: "That's a made-up song!"--in the sense, perhaps, of an original composition. While it is common enough for someone to compose original variations on themes (Leroy Carr's "In the Evening" as the basis for Robert Johnson's "Love In Vain"), Dunbar was claiming to his listeners that he had composed Big Joe

Williams' "Baby, Please Don't Go," which was more a sign of naiveté than dishonesty. He was too naive to understand how crooked the claim sounded to others.

When Dunbar had finished, the listeners scraped together whatever they could to pay him for his time ($50 or so) and took off for New Orleans.

CHAPTER VI: ROGER & GEORGE, ROBERT JR. LOCKWOOD

All through the later 1950s, Roger and George admired Robert Jr. Lockwood as they listened to WAOK. They did not know that they admired Lockwood, since they had no discographies to tell them that the smooth and funky guitarist on Sonny Boy Williamson's "Cross My Heart" or "Your Funeral, My Trial" was, in fact, he, but they listened to that guitar player with real appreciation. In Lockwood's years as a session player at Chess Records in Chicago, he had made many standard Chicago blues into something quite unique and often sublime. The Candid sides that Lockwood cut with Otis Spann in New York in 1960 are masterpieces of interwoven textures--of inter-play that transcends the notion of "lead" and "accompaniment." Though he's never been as famous as most of his comparably talented contemporaries, Robert Lockwood, Jr. is an artist to whom history will be very kind.

Robert had moved to Cleveland in 1960. He had moved to Cleveland from Chicago in the belief that it would be better for his family, and he actually gave up music for a time, working only a day job on a delivery truck for a pharmacy. It was not too long before he began to play again, though now in the decidedly unlucrative Cleveland market, and he formed a trio that consisted of the sax player Maurice Reedus and the bassist Gene Schwartz. When Roger went to Hiram College, a liberal arts school some forty miles southeast of Cleveland, in 1973, Robert had been in the area for about thirteen years, and because he'd left Chicago he'd pretty much lost any chance for a large following of the kind enjoyed by Buddy Guy or Muddy.

It was soon after Roger arrived at Hiram that George called to tell him that he was going to collaborate on a documentary that was being filmed on Lockwood, and he invited Roger, his wife Germaine, and a guest to come along to meet Robert. Roger asked Seth Carlin, a colleague in the Music Department at Hiram, to come along and they and their wives set out for Cleveland one evening to meet George and the film crew at a Howard Johnson's motel.

When they arrived in Cleveland the scene was a bit odd. They went in to the Howard Johnson's restaurant and they discovered that the crew was German. The head of the film crew was sitting at the counter drinking coffee and he was a fairly humorless type. He greeted the arriving Mitchell party with a cold look and said that this simply would not do: he announced immediately, and much to the chagrin and amazement of all concerned, that there would be "no girls" allowed to accompany them! He insisted that Lockwood would "clam up" if there were any women present and thus he gave Roger and Carlin a choice to make--and one minute in which to make it, since they were running behind: come, and leave your wives behind; leave now, with your wives, and forfeit the chance to see Lockwood. The upshot is that Roger and Carlin went to see Robert, but not without plenty of anxiety about how their wives would greet them on their return.

They drove across some of the worst of Cleveland's Hough area slums to find Robert's house, which is in a middle class black neighborhood, and when they arrived there Robert's wife, Anne, greeted them at the door. Anne is a very protective wife, rather younger than Robert himself, and she takes very good care of him. She asked them all in and the visitors sat down and watched the proceedings. Robert sat in a chair and warmed up, running some chords and riffs to get loose. Carlin, the professor of music, was impressed simply by the warm-ups--this was just as well, since there was little music and lots of technical stuff from the crew. They left after a bit, glad to have met Lockwood, but nervous about their wives. The wives awaited them, none too patiently, at the Howard Johnson's and Germaine told Roger what she thought of the German film crew. Lockwood, himself, of course, scoffed at the notion.

It was not long after this affair of the abandoned wives that Pete Lowry, with whom Roger had made the rounds in Atlanta in 1971, called to say that he was going to do a Lockwood album on his Trix label and wondered if he could use Roger's place in Hiram as a headquarters and use Roger as a collaborator. Pete said it would take only a couple of days. It soon became a week.

The first day of recording was done in Roger's house in Hiram, and since Hiram is in the middle of the country, Roger had worried whether the trio from Cleveland could find his house. To this, Robert responded: "We're musicians. We can find anything!" The session began with Robert sitting in Roger's chair and the equipment rolling. It was a hot July day, Robert was playing with great intensity, and the room was fairly stifling. As Robert spun out intense versions of "Little Boy Blue" and "Mr. Down Child," "Dust My Broom" and "Lonely Man," the sweat ran down his head and soaked his shirt. His body swayed in time to the music, his playing was brilliant and his singing as fine as ever. Given the conditions, someone asked Robert if he'd like to take a break and he answered, in a knowing double entendre: "No! Lemme go while I'm hot!"

The next session was at Robert's house in Cleveland and the results were just as edifying: hot versions of "Funny, But True," "Annie's Boogie," "Driving Wheel," and a jazzy "Majors, Minors and 9ths." Robert was putting all of his cards on the table, so to speak, and the hand was impressive. The recording began in the early evening and went until about 1:00 A.M. They did some of the songs in a couple of takes, but on others it was hard to satisfy everyone. Maurice Reedus, during the taping of one song, could not satisfy himself. They would play the song, Lowry would play it back, and Reedus would shake his head. "Naw--I gotta put a little more soul in that!" They did around fifteen takes before Reedus was satisfied.

Reedus was a bit of a card, in addition to matching Robert's perfectionism. During the taping, Roger sat by the door and at one point, knowing that Roger was from the South, Reedus called out in his general direction: "Hey, boy, close that door!" well aware that these were fighting words when a white man said them to a black man. Just before Reedus could deliver his punch-line ("I don't see anyone moving, so I guess we're all men here!"), Roger called back, in mock fury, "Who you callin' 'boy'!" Robert smiled a very large smile at this exchange, and Reedus and Roger both laughed. In an atmosphere of perfectionism, a bit of joking is often a fine release.

It was also this night that a friend of Robert's came over with some moonshine and Robert decided that Roger should drink some. Not being much of a drinker, Roger politely declined. Robert was in a clowning mood, however, and he insisted that Roger drink the hooch. He put on a threatening face, and being a big, tough guy, when Robert closed on Roger and said: "You're gonna drink it or wear it, one!" Roger meekly drank it down, not at all pleased with the results.

When the LP was finally issued on Trix (it is no longer available, but one hopes it will eventually come back into print), it was called *Contrasts*, because of the contrasting jazzy and bluesy styles, the acoustics and electrics, the solos and the trios. There is a fine version of the Roosevelt Sykes tune "Driving Wheel" on the LP that almost didn't make it on. The tune was played on Lowry's Gibson, and Roger and Pete disagreed about the song: Pete thought the strings were too heavy; Roger had always liked the song very much and liked this version. After some talk back and forth they agreed to leave it on and so much the better, since it's a very nice piece. The title is, in many ways, a weak one, says Roger, since it does not identify the material well. Anne Lockwood was quite angry with the title and she could not understand why it was not named after "Little Boy Blue."

After the *Contrasts* LP, Roger and Germaine had the Lockwoods to dinner and the Lockwoods had them to dinner. After the dinner in Cleveland, Roger offered to take Robert's visiting mother (who always, and only, called him "Junior," by the way) back to the airport for him, and Robert agreed. Mrs. Lockwood was an elderly lady and, though she was a share-cropper's daughter born in the 19th century, and one can only assume that her opportunities for education and refinement were very limited, she was still a very refined and elegant lady. It was to this lady that Roger wanted to put a particular question: what was it like to live with Robert Johnson? In the informal circumstances of impoverished peoples, marriage and its expenses was not always an option, so what later became known as "living together," among middle class people, was common. Robert Lockwood, Jr. thus grew up with Robert Johnson as an informal step father, and Roger wanted to ask Mrs. Lockwood about Johnson but was swayed from asking by her dignity. Roger also recalls that the first thing he said to Mrs. Lockwood was: "You must be proud to have such a talented son." To this, she replied in an almost 19th century manner: "The buttons are bursting off my vest!"

In 1974, the year after the *Contrasts* LP, Roger helped arrange a concert at Hiram College for Robert's trio. The location was Hayden Auditorium, which holds three hundred people, and Roger was excited to get Robert some recognition in the area, where he is vastly under-appreciated. Roger's part was mostly to convince Robert to play, and not to engineer the mechanics of the concert, its promotion and so on. It was too late, then, that Roger noticed that the student activities board, which was supposed to advertise the show, had basically done nothing to promote it at all. When the trio arrived there had been a few hastily posted notices, but little else, and there were about twenty people in the auditorium. Roger was furious with the guy who was supposed to have handled the promotion and to this day is angry with "the guy who dropped that ball." The trio, Robert, Gene and Maurice, were probably used to such botched shows, and barely even expressed any notice of it--they really rocked the people who did show and Roger was very pleased with the results of the performance, if not with the attendance. Roger was apologetic, Robert was gracious, and there seemed to be no problem--as old pros, the trio had played a good show for the pay upon which they had agreed and they held no grudges.

It was in the next year that the Muddy Waters Band came to the same Hayden Auditorium at Hiram College, and this time the student activities board actually advertised the show. When Roger found out that Muddy was in town, he immediately called Robert to tell him about it. Muddy and Robert were both fixtures on the Chicago scene in the 1950s, so it was a chance for them to say hello. When Roger got Robert on the phone, the latter told him to go tell Muddy that he was coming down to Hiram. Roger went over to the auditorium that afternoon and Muddy and the band were sitting around playing cards and killing time. Roger introduced himself to them and then said: "Robert Lockwood asked me to tell you that he's coming tonight." Muddy just said: "Yeah, I know. He called me." Roger laughed, a bit embarrassed, and had his picture taken with Muddy while he had the chance (it didn't come out!). Muddy had a cold, so wasn't in very good form, but the band played for a while before he came out, he reeled off a few tunes, and the audience seemed happy with the result. Muddy and Robert reminisced a bit after the show, telling stories and laughing.

It was 1984 that Roger next saw Robert at the 1984 music festival in Atlanta organized by George Mitchell with plenty of big names: Sonny Terry, Homesick James, Henry Townsend, Robert Lockwood, Jr. It was also the occasion on which the death of Buddy Moss was announced to the public. Roger, as an old friend of the organizer, was given free entrance, access to the backstage area, and even to the performers' keg. He went to greet Robert after a gap of ten years, saying: "Hi, Robert! I'm Roger Brown. Remember me from Hiram?" and was surprised to receive a complete brush-off. Robert gave him a very limp handshake and about the dirtiest look he'd ever gotten. When Robert Lockwood wants to chill you, he can really put on the freeze (I got one of these freezes when I tried to talk to Lockwood at a performance at Cat Fish Blue in Cleveland in the 1990s when I was writing this book – he just turned sour and turned off!). Roger was confused, since they'd left on such friendly terms. He left Robert and talked to some other people.

    The next night the situation shifted. Anne Lockwood saw Roger and greeted him as a long lost friend, giving him a big hug, and then Robert began to loosen up a bit. What had caused the chill was not long in coming: Robert had agreed to do a video with someone at Hiram College and the person had never paid him for it. Robert was never rolling in the dough and had been ripped-off in many a record deal, so non-payment of that sort really angered him. He was so angry with the guy at Hiram, in fact, that the entire college, including Roger, who had been at the University of New Hampshire since 1977, came to be an object of his hatred. Roger had been guilty by association, for a time, but this seemed to wear off after a bit. He wore a tee shirt that displayed another Lockwood Trix LP, *Robert Junior Lockwood Does 12*, and perhaps this made Robert less angry with him. They parted on friendly terms.

    In 1988, Roger saw Robert again, this time in Portsmouth, New Hampshire. For someone who doesn't read newspapers much, it was a bit of a surprise simply to grab a local paper by chance and see that Robert was playing in near-by Portsmouth that night. He got his wife, Bonnie, and some friends together and got down there in a hurry. When they arrived, Roger found Anne Lockwood by the stage, ever vigilant, and put his hands over her eyes while saying hello. They had a very pleasant visit, and Robert announced to the crowd that his old friend "Mr. Rogers" was there to see him! They spoke briefly at break and Robert was amused that Roger, who lives in a country area of New Hampshire after living in a country area of Ohio, was still living out in the sticks.

The last time Roger saw Robert was at the 1992 opening of the Cambridge, Massachusetts House of the Blues. This was an invitation only performance which also included Henry Townsend and David "Honey Boy" Edwards, and Roger was invited with his wife and allowed two guests. Since he was teaching a course at the University of New Hampshire on blues at the time, he decided that he would use his other tickets to take a couple of students from the class with him. They drew two names from a hat and these two accompanied Roger down to Boston to hear Robert play.

On the way down, Roger remembers that one of the students asked him, rather sheepishly, if he thought that Robert would play his favorite tune, "Driving Wheel." Roger, who remembered having to fight to keep the number on the *Contrasts* LP, was amused to have it come up again and said he'd see what he could do. Before the show, Roger went up to talk to Robert and Anne for a couple of hours. One of the tidbits that Roger remembered from their discussion was that Robert said that Sonny Boy Williamson's friends called him "WM," presumably for "Willie Miller." It was that sort of friendly discussion where odds and ends are dropped in a pleasant atmosphere. Roger mentioned, in passing, that one of the students really liked "Driving Wheel" and hoped that Robert would play it. Robert thought for a second and said with finality: "I'll play it for him." He put on a great show, as usual, and the student was thrilled that Robert had paid attention to his request.

One of the things that Roger remembers well from talking with Robert is the vast difference in their attitudes to Will Shade. Roger was always very fond of Will and remembered him as the first bluesman ever to play for him. Will was always very courteous and generous in his dealings with Roger and George, and as far as Roger was concerned, he was a great guy. The business at Bo Carter's house in Memphis had given him a feel for the ideas other people had of Will, but Roger's attitudes had not really changed much because of it. When Roger brought up Will and Charlie Burse to Robert in the 1970s, however, Robert had expressed his fondness for Charlie Burse, but had exploded at the mention of Will's name.

Apparently, sometime in the late 1950s or early 1960s, Robert had been in Memphis while touring and Will Shade had offered to put him up. Old organizer that he was, Will had also arranged for a woman to keep the bachelor Robert company. Robert, however, not having been born the day before, was cautious and spread his money out under the bathroom mat before bed.

Robert was awakened in the morning by Will and the woman speaking in those loud whispers that are supposed by the speakers to be inaudible to others. He was appalled to hear Will arguing with the woman about Robert's money! She was supposed to roll Robert, take his money, and share it with Will, but she'd gotten not a cent. He recalls the punch line to their argument when she said: "Son of a bitch ain't got any money!" Robert gathered his money and left, no longer a pal of Will's, to be sure.

Another fine bit of Lockwoodiana was the story Robert told Roger about his tour in Memphis. Robert was on Beale Street eating at one of the cafeteria-style places that had come to dominate the former sin zone in the post war era. He put his lunch on a tray and put it on a table and went off to get his drink. When he returned, there was a guy in ragged clothes and a scraggly beard eating his lunch. Robert just put down the drink for him and went back to get himself another lunch. Maurice Reedus, who was there for the telling of the story, commented on the man: "He was hungry!"

It was a few years later, in another city where Robert had a gig, that Robert was stopped by a well-dressed, successful man who shook his hand and thanked him for the lunch that day. He said that his luck had changed and he gave Robert the royal treatment that day--gave him the key to the city, remembering well his kindness back in Memphis.

CHAPTER VII: RAY FLERLAGE, "OUTRAGEOUS AND WEIRD"

At age 80, Ray Flerlage seems more like a youthful, rather outrageous, 60 year-old than he does an elderly man born in 1915. His eyes sparkle with enthusiasm, his voice is clear, and he has just finished devouring the novels of Anthony Trollope. Though he is known among blues people mostly for his photography, the first quarter hour I spent with Ray Flerlage revealed great enthusiasms for English literature, music of all sorts, tea, wine (now forbidden by the doctor), and cooking. The first half hour also revealed a great lifelong enthusiasm for the company of attractive ladies and an enthusiasm for inter-racial relations that dates back to the 1940s.

After speaking to him for a few hours about his conservative parents, his rebellious enthusiasm for the company of black people during a period of strict segregation, his two marriages to black women, his fifty years living in Chicago's black community, and his general refusal to accept the conventional norms around him, I was unable to resist saying to him that it's almost bizarre that he had these inter-racial interests when he did. "Until twenty-five years ago," I laughed, "it would have been outrageous and weird!"

Not even remotely offended, he looked at me and chuckled. He said calmly: "Uh-huh...Yeah, I mean, that could be your lead-in to my segment: outrageous and weird!" And, indeed, it could because Ray is entirely his own man.

Ray and I had planned to meet at B Side Records, a used and rare shop on 53rd Street in Hyde Park that displays some of his work, but Ray's watchful and protective wife, Louise, put the nix on that when the ice gained a thin covering layer of snow. Ray has lost his balance due to a bungled operation and he has to make his way around with two canes. People without that handicap were already slipping and sliding around in Keystone Kops fashion, so he was instructed by Louise to stay put. Directions were given to the Flerlage home over the phone, and we met there, in a predominantly black neighborhood on 67th Street, about an hour later.

It was from 1959 to 1975 that Raeburn Flerlage took some of the most memorable photographs remaining to us documenting the

Chicago blues scene. His 1967 photos of Howlin' Wolf in action over an evening at Silvio's on the West Side are almost unique in capturing the power of Wolf's performances, and Flerlage' s style, dark and action-oriented, is readily recognizable. A cursory glance through the many items written on Chicago blues since the mid-1960s will also find Ray Flerlage' s name in the majority of the acknowledgments. As a photographer, as a guide, and as a source of information, Ray has been an important figure in Chicago's blues history.

When you talk to Ray Flerlage today, however, he seems a bit taken aback by all the attention. Since the explosion of interest in blues around 1990, he has suddenly been bombarded with requests to use his photos for various books and CDs and by requests to talk to him about his career as a photographer. He sold over one hundred photos in a six month period of 1995 alone, and people from a blues magazine have been around to get him to produce an autobiographical sketch. Having been forced since 1975 by the deteriorating social conditions of the South and West Sides (caused in particular by drug wars) to avoid the clubs, Flerlage has not snapped a shot in twenty years. But twenty years later he is experiencing his own personal renaissance.

*

Raeburn Flerlage was born in 1915 in Cincinnati, Ohio (which he pronounces like a native: "Cincinnata"). "...I came up in what you might call an Archie Bunker-type family." His father was "highly prejudiced in all areas where prejudice is identifiable," and all ethnic groups were referred to by the proper term of racist opprobrium. Flerlage looks back at his father as a man with some good qualities, such as being hard-working and responsible, but the strong biases and prejudices of the father were not shared by the son. "...[H]e and I always had very different ideas" is how he puts it now, but one can imagine that the disagreements between the "outrageous and weird" son and the Archie Bunker father were stronger than that.

Flerlage thinks of his life as having changed significantly while he was in high school from 1930 to 1934. He initially attended a Protestant high school and his interests were primarily physical. He was a boxer, a weight-lifter, and a brawler, and he was forced to leave the Protestant high school when he took a swing at the principal there--this forced him to attend a Catholic school. Though he was the same brawler at the Catholic school at first, things changed when "I ran into an instructor who found that I had a brain. And the first year there I underwent...a metamorphosis. I became a mental person." Suddenly, the brawler was literary editor, on the debate team, and so on. When Flerlage graduated from high school in 1934 he worked where he could for a while until he landed a job on the *Cincinnati Post* in the later 1930s.

Starting almost immediately after high school, Ray Flerlage began what was to be a constant theme through almost the whole of his adult life: he began writing articles and reviews of books and music. Demonstrating that a high school education in 1934 meant a whole lot more than one in 1994 Flerlage says:

"I was doing this record review column called 'The Magic Groove,' and I was very hungry for records. I would review anything! I would review Bruckner's 7th Symphony and Mahler's 9th--as a matter of fact, I wrote a national article on Gustav Mahler before anyone knew who Gustav Mahler was (that is regular, everyday people)--we're talking about 1941. I remember the article: 'America and Gustav Mahler'...But I would also...review Josh White's 'Chain Gang Blues,' and Key Note Records, the Almanac Singers, and 'Talking Union'..." With no money and a real hunger for records, Flerlage reviewed avidly to build a collection that would satisfy him.

Though, as stated above, Ray Flerlage has lived in the black community of Chicago for fifty years and he has been married to two black women, in his early life in Cincinnati he had no real exposure to black Americans. His first significant exposure to a black person was through interviews conducted with the singer Marian Anderson in about 1942 and Paul Robeson a year or so after. Flerlage even had the pleasure of having Marian Anderson make a record at his suggestion: he told her how much he liked the 'Lament of Dido' in Purcell's Dido and Aneaus and how perfect her voice was for it, and she proceeded to record a version soon thereafter. His only regret was that she used a piano accompaniment and not the string orchestra he thought would have been perfect.

This time on the *Cincinnati Post*, however, was to be interrupted by the outbreak of World War II. Flerlage was 27 when the US had entered the war in earnest and he knew that he would not be called up immediately because they wanted the 18 year-old boys first. But one way potentially to avoid the draft was to work in war industry.

"At that time in Cincinnati--this was wartime and I was married and had three children--and I was advised that it would be wise if I went to a war plant and saw if anything was available there...I went out to Wright Aeronautical and was interviewed and I tried to center on practical things in my background, of which there were very few because I'm not a practical person--all my interests were sort've arty. I was writing record columns and all that kinda stuff, largely to get free records...After about 15-20 minutes of the interview and I'd told them all of the things I can do...and they said: 'Look, what we're looking for is somebody who knows music, and we were told that you know music. We're looking for someone to run a music program here in the war plant.'"

As it turned out, Flerlage was given the Stalinist-sounding title Director of Industrial Music for the plant and the job consisted not in the drudgery he had been expecting, but in playing music through the sound system. This was a job he liked. Not only was he programming music, but he was also able to trade his free records he'd gotten for writing columns for ones he wanted at stores or at work. He might give the plant a Glenn Miller and trade at the shop for a Leadbelly.

Part of the job of the Director of Industrial Music was also employee recreation. "I supervised the organization of employee music groups: choruses, small orchestras, jazz groups and so forth, the most effective of which were black." Though he had spoken to Marian Anderson this was a different experience. "This was about my third major exposure across the color lines." The second had been his dealings with black executives in the plant.

In the wartime operation of the plant, black men in segregated Cincinnati were permitted to act as executives, presumably because skilled leadership was required but in short supply. Flerlage was a member of the Executive Committee and there was predictable trouble on the committee because of the unwillingness of the white executives to take the black executives seriously. Though there were integrated meetings many of them were also segregated, and Flerlage resented the demeaning attitudes towards his black counterparts that were adopted in the segregated ones. His displeasure with the other whites alienated him from them, of course, and they designated him as the token white at black social functions. Far from resenting this designation, Ray began to enjoy the company of his black colleagues and their families and he began "to visit their homes and got to know them quite well. As a matter of fact, it caused me some problems because I met some very lovely girls, too. But clear back then in the 1940s I started to get into the black community."

In around 1944, Flerlage and his first wife decided to go to Chicago where she had grown up. He left his job as Director of Industrial Music at Wright Aeronautical willingly enough, partly because it looked as if he might be drafted anyway. Soon after coming to Chicago he was again involved in music: "I came up here and started giving lectures on folk music called 'The People and Their Music' at the Parkway Community House. As a result of that exposure, there [were some] people who attended that had some affiliation with the relatively new People's Songs, Inc., and I was offered the job of Midwest Executive Secretary." This was around 1947.

People's Songs was founded in the basement apartment of the famous folk singer Pete Seeger in Greenwich Village on December 31, 1945. Though a number of the thirty people present at the founding were members of the Communist Party, most were not: they were folk singers, chorus directors, union education officials, and others who were concerned both with music and with progressive politics. Their idea for People's Songs had little to do with the Communist Party and its preoccupation with ideological purity and loyalty to the Party line. They wanted to create an entity in which old folk songs could be sung, new folk songs written, and solidarity created with like-minded colleagues. They wanted to place the music in the service of unions for rallies and picket lines and hoped that the presence of peoples' songs in everyday life would create feelings of solidarity in a society dominated by commercial music that promoted passivity in listeners, not a desire to be producers of music themselves.

The early leading members of People's Songs, such as Woody Guthrie, Ronnie Gilbert and Pete Seeger, were all basically unorthodox Communists who paid little attention to the ideological struggles among Party ideologues and worked out their own view of the world. People's Songs reflected the idea that folk culture could act to unite the exploited and disinherited in a common cause, and all the while speaking a language derived not from Comintern pronouncements or capitalist marketing and advertising, but from the language of popular (folk) culture itself. They started the music publishing venture, a magazine for those who joined the organization, a booking agency, and branches of the organization in other cities outside New York.

People's Songs raised money for the organization by organizing concerts, sing-alongs, and tours for musicians such as Leadbelly and Josh White, as well as Seeger and Guthrie themselves. They organized classes on music and political action and sponsored lectures like those given by Ray Flerlage in Chicago. In general, they believed, rather naively, that music would express the highest aspirations of the common people and that these highest aspirations would lead them politically out of thrall to the oppressive status quo of American conservatism.

People's Songs survived only three years. If the coming of the Cold War and McCarthyism were proof enough that most Americans would come to speak the language of mass media and conservative ideology, not of folksy solidarity against the grasping capitalist, it was also evident that folk music was not going to mobilize the people. Seeger and Guthrie would continue their work as popular activists and folk singers for years to come, but not under the auspices of People's Songs.

Though he recalls being made Midwest Executive Secretary, Flerlage simply cannot recall, specifically, how he came to be involved with People's Songs. He was not politically active in Cincinnati, though he says that he has always been "pro-underdog." He does recall meeting a leftist novelist named Jack Conroy who'd written a well-respected proletarian novel called *The Disinherited*. Conroy worked for a publishing company in the Loop, on Randolph St., when Flerlage worked at a record store on W. Washington St. They used to eat lunch together from time to time, and Flerlage recently ran across a note in his diaries that indicated that Conroy had given a series of lectures at the Parkway Community House before he did his own series on folk music and also that Conroy had introduced him when he spoke. "I don't think Jack had any connection with People's Songs, but Jack was a left-wing writer, [and] people saw them as a left-wing group." Flerlage thinks that Conroy may have introduced him to other local leftists and that his name may have gotten back to the People's Songs folks.

Though he is not sure how it is any more that he came to be involved with People's Songs, black music and the left, "A lot of these things would have come about because I sought connections with progressive groups and inter-racial groups," he says. Flerlage was divorced and involved with a black woman by the middle 1940s, and he says that it was his desire "to be interracial" that motivated much of what he did (which did not sit well with his father). He also wrote for labor journals during this time, though he doesn't recall being a member of the Communist party, much as he was involved with activities associated with them.

As Midwest Executive Secretary, then, Flerlage promoted concerts with Big Bill Broonzy and others, fund-raisers and so on. "The first people that we had come to Chicago came not to give concerts but to give a party, actually. We were giving a concert with Josh White but we brought to the city Leadbelly and Woody Guthrie. I don't recall that we had a car at that time--I think we must have been in a cab--Studs Terkel, Win Strockey and I. Since I knew the South Side and was living in the black community (as I have ever since) I was asked to find Leadbelly a hotel. Everything was completely segregated then so I had to find him a South Side hotel. So, I guess we were all in a cab with Woody Guthrie and Leadbelly--Woody was harassing Leadbelly, being his usual irascible self, and we got to the room and went up and started to unpack. I told Leadbelly: 'Ya know, I've got a lot of your records...but I've never been able to find 'TB Blues.' So, he keeps on unpacking and everybody's talking and so on, and all of a sudden I realize that Leadbelly's standing there looking at me with his 12-string guitar in his hand singing 'Too late, too late, too late'--he sings me 'TB Blues'!"

Though Flerlage regarded People's Songs as a good cause, he was having a hard time making a living working for them. He made $30 a week when things were going well and when things were rough they just owed him. In 1948, Flerlage handed his job over to Bernie Azbell, who was able to supplement his income by working as a folk singer, and started a new job at a local record store as a "Consultant on Building a Record Collection." He was a record store clerk before too long, a job which included being the buyer for the store. He worked in record retail stores for about three years before another opportunity presented itself, this time through his father (with whom he was on speaking terms again): he began work for five years as a dining car steward on the New York Central Railroad.

After his stint as a steward Flerlage made the switch to being a record wholesaler in 1955, which he continued to do until 1984. He worked for one company until they folded, then began his own. Wholesaling appealed to Flerlage: he made his own hours and this left him free to work on another dream of his which was to teach English literature. Flerlage has always been a polymath and he began to take classes in English at the Chicago Teachers College when he was already about 40. He never completed the course but this did nothing to slow down his reading.

At about the same time he was attending lectures at the Teachers College, Flerlage was also writing articles for newspapers and *FM Guide* when he was approached by a man who said: "Look, anyone can write articles--not everyone can run radio programs. I would like for you to do a radio program for us." This invitation resulted in a radio program on WXFM in 1955 and this show bloomed into shows on WXRT and WSBC as well. Flerlage had shows called "Blues International," "Wednesday Meeting House," "Folk City," "Critics Choice," and "Jazz Journal" on the air at various times between 1955 and 1970.

Ray Flerlage retired from his wholesale business in 1984 and has used his time to continue his voracious reading, his cooking, his sampling of teas, and many other interests, passions and curiosities.

CHAPTER VIII: RAY FLERLAGE AND PHOTOGRAPHY

In the midst of launching his radio shows, writing his reviews, and working in his wholesale business, Ray Flerlage also discovered photography. The immediate inspiration for Ray to take up photography was not a desire to photograph blues musicians, but the fact that he admired the photographs of a sister-in-law of an old girlfriend of his. He went out and bought some expensive cameras and equipment (where he got the money he does not recall) and had his first job taking pictures at a fashion show a friend gave at her home.

These fashion photos were not the wave of the future for him, however. Beside the fact that he was never comfortable working with posed models, his passion for music kept him in touch with some people who would be important in starting him out as a photographer of jazz and blues musicians.

The man who gave Flerlage his first professional job as a photographer was the record company executive Moe Asch, who is quite a story himself. Asch was born in 1905 in Poland. He came from a family of Jewish intellectuals who had left Poland in 1912 to go to Paris, the intellectual center of the Continent, where Marc Chagal was a regular visitor at his home. His family emigrated to the United States in 1914 and after they discovered that the opportunities for leftist Jewish intellectuals were slim in New York, they returned to Paris in 1923. Asch himself, after rejoining his parents in Paris, was sent to study electronics in Germany, where he also became interested in folk music. Asch then moved back to the US not long after reading John Lomax's *Cowboy Songs* in 1925. Asch free-lanced as an electrical engineer in various New York studios for years before setting up his own label, called Asch Records, in 1939. His interest in folk music is evident in his first record, by the Bagelman Sisters, and in the fact that he began to record Leadbelly in 1941.

Asch issued music on his Asch label, but this was supplemented later by Disc Records, Stinson Records, and the eventual replacement of Asch Records, Folkway Records, on which most of the Leadbelly reissues were released in the late 1940s and 1950s. Asch's entrepreneurial spirit was impressive, but so was his dedication to progressive political movements: he supported People's Songs generously for as long as it existed. Asch continued to be active in the music business, always as an extremely independent man, until his death in 1986.

Ray Flerlage had known Asch slightly even as early as his Cincinnati days when he was writing his music review column, "The Magic Groove." He had corresponded with many companies looking for records and while a huge corporation might have an underling respond to him, with Asch Records, as with Folkways, to correspond with the company was to correspond with Moe Asch. Then, while Flerlage was with People's Songs, Asch "furnished us with a lot of records to auction off--trying to raise enough money to pay me $30 a week, the rent, and stuff like that. And yet, he was the first tough businessman I ever knew who just wrote off some money when we couldn't pay. He just [said]: 'Forget it, forget it!'"

Flerlage didn't see much of Asch until after his tour of duty as a dining car steward, when he began as a record wholesaler with Folkways as one of his clients. It was in the middle 1950s that Asch began to come to Chicago for record conventions and contacted Ray to help him at his Folkways booth. "Moe would come into town and--he was the greatest conventioneer, I guess, of modern times. Every kind of convention, he'd be at with Folkways Records." Ray sat at the booth while Asch was out, helped him set up, and so on, and they began to go back to the Flerlage apartment afterwards to talk and have dinner.

Things were pleasant between them and Flerlage began to show Moe Asch some of his photos. Asch, inexplicably, told Ray that his future lay in fashion photography but this was a future that Ray was surely aware was not to be his! Ray was also drawing a small salary from Folkways to act as a promoter and he managed to increase their sales by having Asch interviewed by Studs Terkel, among other things.

It was not always a pleasure working for Asch, however. As one would suspect of so complex and independent a character, Asch was not always completely reasonable. "He could be very unpleasant, very demanding and very difficult...I remember on one occasion he was being so unpleasant that I just got up and walked out. I said 'Moe, I don't have to take this abuse. I don't have to take it.' And no sooner did I hit the door than he came after me. It was just that he was feelin' mean, so he was mean!" [laughs]

His relations with Asch being sufficiently close, it was Asch who gave him his first professional job as a photographer. Asch sent a telegram to Flerlage in 1959 telling him to get to work: Memphis Slim was at the Pershing Hotel in Chicago and he was preparing to go to Europe soon thereafter. Asch asked Flerlage to contact Slim and get some pictures for a couple of Folkways Memphis Slim albums that were yet to be released. Ray jumped at the opportunity.

When he located Slim Ray found him to be a wonderful man. He was patient, friendly, warm and ready to do what it took to get good photographs. They simulated a nightclub atmosphere by placing some glasses and paper cups on the piano and the urbane Slim just played his music. Ray had a girlfriend at the time who was a wonderful pianist and she and Slim took to each other immediately, which helped matters considerably. "Slim gave me his whole day, practically," and the session produced some memorable shots, including some splendid pictures of Slim's hands. Looking at the photos it is hard to describe the effect produced by the long, slender fingers as they worked the keyboard except to say that they are reminiscent of the famous Robert Johnson close-up photograph in which his own slender, almost feminine, fingers are so prominent. Ray tried to describe what he felt about the pictures, but it was difficult for him. In the visual medium, language is not always adequate to convey the impressions made by images. "His hands...long, slim...The most extraordinary hands! I thought of [them as] spider-like..."

These shots of Slim's hands were complemented by a shot that was essentially accidental, but also fascinating to Flerlage and to Asch's art director, Roland Cline. Cline bought "the weirdest picture I have ever sold to anybody in which Slim is sitting there holding his hand up. You can't see who it is--you can't see if it's man or beast. When he ordered it, I couldn't find it." Asch paid him for the photos and gave him a bonus and Ray was hooked on photography for good.

The early photos actually give one a good idea of what would come to be Ray Flerlage's approach in later years. Since he did not like to work with posed models he was no good at posed musicians or even pretty girls. "But if a pretty girl was performing and was worth catching...I've got some gorgeous pictures of Nancy Wilson--she was a pretty girl. Was she ever a fox then!" Mixing his enthusiasms for pretty girls and action photography could produce impressive results, but the pretty girl was, in any event, just a bonus on the job.

"When I was taking pictures of these people in action, and I knew this was what I wanted to do, I would just be watching for what seemed to me to be the visually most exciting, the most communicative, thing. Although I did get...I had to take some pictures of people posing, if they would pose with their instrument, okay, that would be all right. On the other hand I got a couple of jobs that--again--[were] just disastrously lousy! Whenever I look at the job I'm embarrassed as hell."

Among the embarrassments were Billy Boy Arnold and Homesick James. Ray spent much of an afternoon with Arnold, who sat in a room passively holding his harmonica with Ray trying to figure out the best way for him to hold it. Ray had James over to his home, since he wasn't performing anywhere at the time, "and he was embarrassed to be a blues singer. So, he just wanted to sit there with a guitar and smile." With no real idea how to get the posing man to look "visually exciting," little good came out of the sessions for anyone.

Yet, there were also experiences such as that with Johnny Shines. "Johnny Shines, I had a job shooting him and he took me over to Western Hall and got up there on the stage and wailed as long as I wanted. They [the pictures] look like a guy performing because he was performing for me. So, all I feel I was ever good at was catching action, you know, that was like they...like they were!"

But this is not sufficient to explain the distinctive character of much of Flerlage's photography. "The principle thing, if there was something that characterized my pictures, was that I pushed the hell out of the film. You know, in other words, if I went into a place with film rated 400, I'd know darn well that I couldn't get moving figures with 400. So, I figured I was going to call it 1600, then I'd set my camera that way. Pushing the film that much is going to get you a particular kind of picture, and operating on the edge of what's possible is going to get you a darker picture...And so, since I was always operating with the least I could get, my pictures tend to be dark and contrasted."

This pushing of the film created both the dark and contrasted look of the pictures but also an ever so slight graininess that went along well with the feel of the murky dives in which many of the pictures were taken. The graininess also went along with the presence of beer bottles, glasses, cigarettes, and other things one naturally encounters in bars and nightclubs.

"I don't want to see the bottle caps in the corner, necessarily, although there are other things you do want to see, like the top of the piano. At Silvio's you see the clothes and the hats and the bullshit up there and you see the piano strings and all that...You don't need everything, yet I didn't want it to be so neat and organized that they didn't show when a place was crummy, you know? You look at the pictures in Theresa's and it's crummy!"

Flerlage tried to combine a performance scenario with a photographic method that emphasized sparseness and contrast to produce something that would derive benefit from both the setting and his approach to his subject. Dark and sparse photographs of a blues singer performing a tautly emotional song in a dark and dirty bar were effective vehicles for presenting the music in what was then its regular home base.

In 1959 Ray also began to do occasional work for Bob Koester at Delmar (later Delmark) Records. It is not surprising that Ray would come to work for Koester. Ray was a wholesaler and Koester had been one of his customers beginning when Koester still owned Seymour's Record Shop on Wabash Street. When Koester heard from Flerlage that he was now taking pictures he asked him to work for him as a stringer, which is essentially an occasional employee who was unpaid. Koester would use his shots on his records and that exposure would be his payment.

As with his relations to Moe Asch, Ray both liked Koester and found him hard to deal with. Koester gave him lots of work for Delmark, but the pay was never good and Ray found that Koester would often hire other photographers without telling him that he was doing so and their pictures would be competing, often to Ray's detriment. But, Ray would spend time with Koester and though he was never, himself, an "idea man," he says, he was able to help the idea man Koester to fill out his tax forms.

It was in the next couple of years that Ray would meet two important black photographers, Ted Williams and Jim Taylor, who were helpful in getting his career under way. In the early to mid-1960s Ted Williams was getting a lot of *Downbeat* covers and he showed Ray the ropes of the profession. Williams made important contacts for him, such as taking him to see Nancy Wilson, and Williams even passed on to him some opportunities to appear on the cover of *Downbeat* which he could otherwise have had for himself. It was this sort of generosity that also led Williams to introduce Ray to the editor of *Downbeat*, the late Pete Welding, and Welding and Flerlage became good friends as a result. (Williams was also prone to set the now-divorced Ray up with girls he knew--another kindness Ray has not forgotten!)

Jim Taylor was another fine photographer Ray remembers best for an episode that involved a picture Ray had taken of B. B. King. Ray and Taylor were in the darkroom developing the photo when the gregarious Taylor absent-mindedly turned on the light too soon while they were chatting. The photo was ruined, but Flerlage worked on it until he got a decent print with the streaks of light still prominent and then managed to sell it: he represented the streaks as being "diffused by the spotlight," and it was soon used on the cover of Charles Kiel's *Urban Blues*.

Another early part of Ray's photographic training was the annual University of Chicago Blues Festival beginning in 1960. For the next ten years he would go there every year and catch all of the best bluesmen he could. The festival lasted three days and between performances and workshops he could get pictures of a dozen artists. He could find Little Walter and Robert Nighthawk in one session and Buddy Guy, Junior Wells, and Little Walter in another. He would all but live there for the weekend, using his press pass from *Downbeat* to gain entrance to as many places as possible.

When Bob Koester told Ray that having his pictures on albums was a form of payment he was not wrong. After the American Folk Blues Festival began touring Europe in the earlier 1960s, with Koester along on the second tour, the interest in blues in Europe manifested itself in requests from AFBF coordinator Horst Lipmann's request to buy some of his work. Along with requests from the Hot Club in

France and some from England, Flerlage got the idea that once a few of the photos started to appear in various publications suddenly everyone wanted them. He says now that he has been ripped-off plenty since then but that many of the purchasers honored their promises of payment, as well.

It was Pete Welding, however, who provided Ray the opportunity to do what is (arguably) his finest work as a photographer, and that was his Howlin' Wolf series taken on Wolf's home turf at Silvio's on the West Side. The opportunity arose in about 1965 or so (it's a bit vague, now) when Pete Welding went to conduct an interview for *Downbeat* at Wolf's home. "Pete Welding was a very unassuming, unpretentious, guy...Yet, he always seemed to know, in a quiet way, what he wanted to do. He could go into these interviews and get what he wanted." Even with the brusque and imposing Wolf, Welding's charm got the best out of the interviewee.

And with Wolf, his best could be pretty gruff. As Welding questioned Wolf and Wolf responded, Ray took pictures to use for the story. Wolf glared at him the whole time and finally told Ray if he wanted to get some good pictures he should come catch him in action at Silvio's. "I think it was almost a challenge. If I showed you some of the pictures of Wolf during the interview he looked at you, you know, like utter disdain! And I think it might have been a sort of put-down, ya know?" [laughs]

Having lived on the South Side since the middle 1940s, Ray was hardly intimidated by the thought of going to a West Side club, and he accepted the challenge, perhaps surprising Wolf in the process. Not long after the interview Ray, Pete Welding, and Michael Bloomfield all loaded into Ray's car and drove over to catch Wolf at Silvio's.

One of the things Ray always regrets about having been a photographer, rather than just a spectator, was that he was always very busy when he went to catch a performance by someone like Wolf and really didn't have a chance to appreciate the music. "You go into Pepper's with Otis Rush or Muddy Waters. Go into Silvio's with Howlin' Wolf and Hubert Sumlin. Damn, those are experiences!" He had a little fast-winding camera with him and must have shot two hundred and fifty shots that evening at Silvio's, but all the while Ray was missing a spectacular performance.

When Ray arrived and had set up his equipment on a table provided by the owners, Howlin' Wolf was still taking the prerogative of the main attraction to hang out for the first set while his band played. As Ray prepared Wolf's guitarist, Hubert Sumlin, came over to him with a large water glass full of 100 proof bourbon. "Somehow or other I must have told Wolf that I liked bourbon," and Wolf was sure to make him feel at home by providing him the drink of his choice. Ray sipped the whiskey and took some pictures of the band and just before Wolf was ready to take the stage himself he brought over another water glass full of Bourbon.

"I don't recall how far along the first one was, but I thought I was going to be real cool and I said fine, I'd sip it a little bit...I was sippin' on it just a little at a time, thinking I was being very careful, you know, and getting pictures. I guess I realized it was getting to me when I started making eyes at some girls who were making eyes at me. Which...it doesn't make any sense when you're in a club like that taking pictures. At any rate, when I wrapped it all up, got in my car-- then I realized I wanted to go back and see one of those girls...I walked back and the guy at the door says 'I don't think you oughta go back in there.'"

But go back in he did, only to find that the girl had made eyes successfully at someone else. Ray went back to his car, banged off of a couple of supports for the El, and was out of commission until waking up on the lawn the next day with photographic equipment scattered around him. "I think I bothered some people that night," he says under his breath.

For all the drunkenness of his condition the pictures of Wolf are marvelous. The photos capture something of the dynamic energy of Wolf's performance as the leader of the band. With Hubert Sumlin playing stolidly off to the right of the stage and the drummer and bassist perched at the top, one gets a feel for the cramped space in which the set was played by the fact that Wolf's position out front puts him close enough to pound on a table in the audience, should he so desire.

The action is presented beautifully by the details in the pictures: Wolf in his coat and then later, after things had steamed up a little, in only his trademark white shirt; Wolf with his guitar slung over his shoulder and then later playing it; Wolf bent double over the microphone, standing straight and pointing, or down on his knees howling his songs to the crowd. Then there are the folding steel chairs at the tables covered with bottles of Schlitz; the tables immediately before Wolf empty to give him some room to operate; the glare reflecting off of the cheap Howlin' Wolf Band banner behind the drummer's head. The pictures give one a beautiful sense not only for Wolf's performances in Silvio's, but also a sense of Silvio's as a place to perform.

The session produced photos that have been reproduced in many different publications but were not the last time Ray shot photos of Wolf. In another session Ray caught Wolf giving one of his trademark growls and the photo made him look either demonic or beast-like, depending on your take. When the picture appeared in a *Downbeat* article Ray heard from Wolf about it. "Oh, was he pissed! Wolf looked at the picture and said 'I'm no animal!'" There was hell to pay, but Flerlage does recall thinking that it was Wolf's choice to be known as Howlin' Wolf instead of Chester Burnett, and that it was not an entirely inappropriate name for him, after all!

Flerlage was one of the few photographers who spent much time documenting the club scene in Chicago, and he thinks he knows why. "I imagine the reason that there were not an awful lot of photographers wandering around the South and West Side clubs is because you don't...necessarily look for an opportunity to carry a couple of thousand dollars around on your neck by yourself...But I was just comfortable enough in the community--and maybe stupid enough!"

There was a certain understanding implicit in these areas that no one bothered people coming to hear music at the clubs, though that is not always enough to guarantee a peaceful time. At one point Ray was with Chris Strachwitz of Arhoolie Records trying to get some pictures of John Littlejohn and Strachwitz had told him that it would be necessary to use the flash since it was a very dark club.

The session went on for a bit but an irritating scene developed. Every time Flerlage flashed a guy up front would turn and look into the light. "Since he insisted on looking right into the flash it bothered him. So, again, as I say, maybe you can be too comfortable sometimes.

I just assumed that if I got up and walked over to the guy and said: 'Look, you know, give me a break. I'm just going to take a few pictures, we'll be here for fifteen or twenty minutes. I really don't want to bother you, but I have to flash to get the pictures. Just give me a break.' I got up and started to walk towards him, the bartender, seeing me walk toward him and seeing the other guy get up, assumed there was going to be a fight or something. He jumped over the bar, grabbed the other guy, who wasn't doing anything other than looking at me, and threw him out."

Things just got uglier from there. When Flerlage and Strachwitz finally did leave the man was waiting for them outside. He hooked an umbrella around Ray's neck to immobilize him and before things could get any worse, Strachwitz was in the car, turned to Ray and yelled "Get in the car!" and Ray ducked out from under the umbrella and got away.

This is the sort of incident that one would think would be common, but Ray said it was the only time he ever had such a problem. What he recalls more fondly is going to Magic Sam's club on Roosevelt Road, the 1815 Club, with his wife Louise. When they left, on a rather messy winter day, Ray recalls that Sam walked them all the way out to their car "without putting anything on and without covering his billion dollar shoes."

The attack at the club, which was the result of a misunderstanding, was an unusual occurrence. Ray recalls more readily the party given for him and Louise by Little Brother Montgomery. Sunnyland Slim, Big Walter Horton and the German blues scholar Karl Gert zur Heide, who was writing a book on Little Brother, were all there, and it was at this occasion that Little Brother promised to make him and Louise a gumbo someday--which he never did.

*

Ray continued to be associated with Bob Koester through the 1960s, both selling him records at Jazz Record Mart and as a photographer at Delmark Records. Flerlage came to know and like both the harmonica player Charlie Musselwhite and blues enthusiast George Mitchell, both of whom worked in the store. Ray's memories of both of them were that they were likable and unassuming: Musselwhite just smiled when people called him 'Muscle Head," and one of the things that most impressed Ray about Mitchell was how young he was!

Of course, hanging around Delmark meant running into Big Joe Williams. "I knew Big Joe quite well; not terribly much to say about him. I knew him well enough that he could call me up and ask me to run him over to the folk festival, stuff like that...We never went out or anything like that together. I would run into him over at Delmark Records when he sometimes stayed in their basement--stuff like that." Ray remembers that he never experienced the wrong end of Big Joe's famous drunken anger, but that he never had the feelings of warmth and friendship that emanated from someone such as Little Brother Montgomery or Magic Sam.

Joe was always memorable, if not always easygoing: "I remember one funny thing about Joe. At one of the concerts at the Blind Pig, Roosevelt Sykes either had his wife--I don't know what his domestic relations were--or his girlfriend there. And up on the stage, while he was performing...Joe Williams got so damn mad because Syke's girlfriend was not responding to him! It was really funny--he was just mad, boiling mad, and made it clear that's what it was about."

When Ray later talked to Bob Koester about it, wondering if there was more to it than there appeared, Koester told him that Joe was just pissed off because his flirtation was not working and that was the end of the story. "Koester and I have had a funny relationship over the years," says Ray. He was never sure where he stood with Koester and there were misunderstandings over things such as whether hiring Ray to take pictures meant that only he would be hired and whether buying records from Ray's distribution company meant that Koester would not buy from others.

There is one episode in particular that sits on Flerlage's mind concerning a new distributor in town who was living at Koester's place and Koester asked him to give the guy some help getting started. After helping him (and probably without Koester's knowledge), the new guy began raiding Ray's territory. It was not long before Flerlage learned that his warehouse manager was lending the new guy merchandise to sell.

"He would habitually...He would send my warehouse manager upstairs to get change. We had a basement with a retail store on the first floor. Every time, we realized, he would send him up to get change...While he was upstairs getting change, he finally decided to figure out why are you always sending me away? And he looked over the railing every time he went, the guy would go over and go through our books and copy down our accounts and go out and raid them!"

Even after telling Koester that this was going on, Koester, says Ray, didn't seem to believe him--and this simply made Ray wary. After nearly coming to blows at a NAIRD meeting once over a matter of voting procedure he and Koester became slightly cool towards each other. These things pass, however, and the two have been cordial for many years.

*

When I told Ray Flerlage that I was considering adding "When Mr. Charley Met the Blues" as a playful subtitle for this book, he took the "Mr. Charley" reference in quite another spirit than the one intended. While "Mr. Charley" was a name often used by black Americans in the first part of the century to identify a white man whose name they didn't know--"Mr. Charley says thus and such"--Ray took it to mean that he was being associated with white racism. For a man who has lived on the South Side as a part of the black community for fifty years this is very important to him.

"I don't want anyone to think that I fit into Mr. Charley. I was never Mr. Charley. Never thought of myself as Mr. Charley...I'm one of those people who're blessed...to see past the veil. They see the person...I once told [a friend], 'ya know, actually I've always felt more comfortable with people of another race than with my own...I've always been comfortable with blacks--to the exclusion, a lot of times--though I've got a lot of wonderful white friends (and naturally, children, too. I have three wonderful white children, and others who are mixed.)"

The Mr. Charley reference was meant to be more playful than anything, but for Ray Flerlage it was like a challenge, but one that he was more anxious to explain than he was to fight about it. He doesn't need to prove anything, after all, just clarify.

But Ray is not a narrow person who only likes things that are associated with black America--he likes many different things, both in art and in daily life. He was as happy to discover that both he and the German scholar Karl Gert zur Heide liked Earl Grey tea as he was to find that they both loved the music of Little Brother Montgomery.

For Ray, in fact, one of the most important themes he brings up in conversation is metamorphosis. Not only does he recall vividly his own change from a physical to a mental person in the early 1930s, but he recalls a particular instance of metamorphosis very fondly: that of a newly "rediscovered" Son House, in 1964. Ray recalls going to see House at Pete Welding's house in 1964 and noticing that he seemed very subservient--he seemed to be a man of surfaces who just smiled broadly because he had no depths to plumb, no pain to interrupt the smile in the course of the day.

Yet, when House walked onto the stage another man appeared. In his music Son House expressed something deeper that one could not see in his everyday self-presentation. "He would walk onto the stage and you never saw such a transformation in your life. A metamorphosis, I guess you'd say. This is a different creature...Agonizing! Agonizing! If you saw him but didn't recognize truth...Go home! Forget it!"

Truth, honesty, feeling. All of these things go into Ray's idea of what makes something stand outside the normal, the average, the conventional in art. Son House's transformation was great because it expressed a truth about human suffering, about the difference between surfaces and depths, and about the difference between an experience of music and an experience of an individual's conventional speaking and socializing habits. To Ray, the important thing was that he was there to see both sides and to experience the change--to realize the possibilities of change and metamorphosis in yet another time and place.

Even though he loved Son House, it is Otis Spann who is Ray's favorite bluesman and the musician whose music expresses his attitude to music best. He likes Spann not when he is rocking and rollicking in barrelhouse style, but when he plays a long, slow, blues. "If I see an Otis Spann track--six minutes, five minutes, hopefully eight minutes--damn, I'll get it in a minute. It's his slow blues. I just think that's the most gorgeous thing you can listen to." Long, slow songs, with lots of time to work out themes and express changes within the whole--very appropriate to a man who has not only lived for eighty years but has relished changes and incongruities as the essence of life.

CHAPTER IX: BOB KOESTER & DELMARK RECORDS

If you wanted to find Delmark House, the new home office of Bob Koester's Delmark Records, you would have to take the Lakeshore up past the Loop, exit on the near North Side, and then drive for a bit through some non-descript older neighborhoods. Barber shops and mom and pop diners are the kinds of places you see in these neighborhoods, punctuated by an occasional trendy coffee shoppe or a record store. Reading Spanish would often be a help but it would not be a necessity. It's one of those neighborhoods that does not seem to be poor or the ghetto of any one group--but the Range Rovers and the sushi bars just wouldn't fit in that well. They'd be lonely.

Delmark House, on the other hand, seems to fit in just fine. It's down a side street in a row of brick buildings that look like warehouses and the street is wide enough to accommodate a semi going either way at the same time. Delmark House is a small building with plate glass windows at the front that looks a bit like a furniture showroom. There's a place across the street that sells boats, and you can look over through their garage door and see a forklift and a couple of guys laughing as they go about their business, a few large motor boats evident in the background. There is an auto parts place down the street and the street is also a thoroughfare for a neighborhood behind the buildings, sending a few former luxury cars through on their way to the main road.

When you go in to Delmark House it is obvious that the profits are going back in to the music not the offices. There are a couple of old sofas to sit on in the lobby and a reception desk close to the door. You can see a small office (Koester's) off the lobby with papers piled all over the desk, a couple of old typewriters piled on top of each other on a table, and more boxes of papers on the floor. The other offices are similar: messy, but by no means a disaster. They are simply work spaces, not show places, and are untidy in the same way that your study is at home. There is a fine recording studio in the building that frees Koester from using other people's studios for the first time since he started the company in 1953, and a warehouse with boxes of LPs, cassettes and CDs. There was a drum set in the hall outside the studio the day I was there as well as some miscellaneous recording equipment. The building used to house a slide and film company and they left behind them a big machine that converts 35 mm film into 16 mm slides. Koester is fascinated and amused by the machine and wants to figure a way to use it.

The walls in Delmark House are decorated with blown up photos of some Delmark greats: Sleepy John Estes looking much older than he really was; Big Joe Williams sitting in front of a chain link fence with a cigarette and a paper cup of Fresca, his guitar to the side of him and his ample gut in front; a picture of Koester and Big Joe in front of a poster announcing the release of *Hoodoo Man Blues* by Junior Wells, Denmark's best seller. There is also a picture of the street singer Arvella Gray outside the old Jazz Record Mart on Lincoln Street, a paper cup secured around his neck and playing a steel guitar; and a copy of a poster announcing: "Silvio's Presents a Sensational Blues Battle" between "Elmore James and his Broom Dusters and Muddy Waters and his Hoochie Coochie Boys" at Silvio's Lounge on the West Side.

There are two certificates from the Hot Club de France, the prestigious jazz society whose honorary president was Louis Armstrong: one award is to Delmark Records "pour son disque LP *Blues on the Highway* de Big Joe Williams," and this album was given "Grand Prix Mondial du disque de jazz 1963"; the other certificate is "Grand Prix du Disque de Jazz 1971"..."pour son disque *Jimmy Dawkins' Fast Fingers*." These are the only two blues LPs that have ever received these awards from the Hot Club in all of its decades in existence. Koester never mentioned them but he must be proud of the awards. Delmark House, in short, is about the music--not the business of music.

Bob Koester moved Delmark Records to Delmark House in June of 1995. It was the first time since the founding of the label back in St. Louis in 1953 that Delmark was housed separately from Koester's other business, Jazz Record Mart, which is in its own new location downtown at 444 S. Wabash. For forty years Delmark had lived in basements and back rooms in the various locations of Koester's record stores, the label often consisting solely of a couple of desks and a stash of LPs and record jackets.

But even if it has its own place now, Delmark is hardly becoming pretentious. It is still a small business atmosphere and Koester scoffs at what he calls "square business," the corporate approach that is based on the bottom line not on the music. For Koester, one could say in the form of a contemporary cliché, the music is the bottom line and he would rather not record any music than make a ton of money recording commercial junk.

It is odd to think that the founder of this Chicago musical landmark was born and raised in Wichita, Kansas, not in Chicago, and that he studied cinematography, not music, at St. Louis University. Koester's story begins with his love of traditional ("trad") jazz and blossoms out to include blues. But the story really begins not with jazz but with a music that a white kid in Wichita was more likely to hear appreciatively in the late 1930s and 1940s: Western Swing.

*

People interested in blues usually discover in the course of their reading that the mobile recording units for the various northern record companies recorded both "hillbilly" and "race" artists in the South in the 1920s. One does not always consider that the two markets, for rural white and black music, were both new ones, not just the down-home blues. Ralph Peer and Polk Brockman of OKeh were as important in beginning the trade in "hillbilly" records as they were in "race" records (Peer coined both terms), and the explosion of interest in buying both kinds of music was simultaneous.

For a white kid such as Bob Koester, born in Wichita in 1932, the common music of his youth was "hillbilly" music. That a person would come to be interested in jazz through listening to "hillbilly" music is only peculiar if one forgets that the country music great Jimmie Rodgers, born in Meridian, Mississippi in 1897, grew up listening to the blues of his black neighbors and was taught to play guitar and banjo by black workers on the railroad gang on which he worked. The fact that Rodgers recorded with bluesmen such as Clifford Gibson and was generally conversant with the musical repertoire of rural Mississippi blacks in the early part of the century only accentuates the relations between the underclasses of Southern blacks and whites--at least culturally. Though not all country music or musicians were so deeply involved with the music of black Americans it was by no means uncommon.

"Western swing" was a hybrid music of hillbilly, pop, blues and jazz that was played by a descendant of the fiddle-based hillbilly string band, the latter exemplified by Brockman and Peer's discovery Fiddlin' John Carson. Western Swing developed in the Southwest among white hillbilly musicians who also played jazz--they had altered the string band from one based in fiddle with guitars and banjos for rhythm to one that was more like a jazz orchestra. They added improvisational approaches to instrumentals, the steel guitar and often the piano and the tenor sax. The music tended to be instrumental and was basically a form of dance music that was heard on the radio, juke boxes, and in dance halls around the Southwest.

The recorded repertoire of one prominent western swing band, Milton Brown's Musical Brownies (on labels with prominent "race" series, Bluebird and Decca), includes jazz and blues classics such as "St. Louis Blues," "Memphis Blues," and "Joe Turner Blues." The guitarist from Bob Wills' influential Texas Playboys recorded (and copyrighted!) a tune called "Steel Guitar Rag" that was essentially a reworking of the bluesman Sylvester Weaver's 1923 OKeh side "Guitar Rag." The Texas Playboys also recorded "St. Louis Blues" and "Trouble in Mind," as was common for any Western Swing band. Western Swing had become very popular and well-defined by the beginning of the 1940s as a music for dancing, and the radio, which had become an important medium in broadcasting hillbilly music in the 1930s, also spread the music to those not at the dance hall.

Koester says that the Western Swing bands were not all ones that he could stand to hear now: "Bob Wills wasn't as bad as some of the others" is about the highest praise he can conjure up today. He recalls hearing the KFA Chart Valley Boys in their weekly Thursday broadcast and he liked them well enough to go see them in person. The broadcast was a strange one, he says, with a fat hillbilly comedian named Edgar Winterbottom and a ragtime pianist also featured with the Chart Valley Boys.

Listening to these bands put into Koester's mind an interest in the jazz side of their music and this he was able to explore on the radio and on records. By the 1930s and early 1940s it was common for jazz to be treated seriously by the white and black middle classes, and the first book on the subject, *Jazzmen*, edited by Fred Ramsey and Charles Smith, came out in 1939. To hear traditional New Orleans jazz played by the masters of the genre was thus fairly easy and there were discographies and re-issues that made the personnel knowable and the recordings available. A mark of the times was that the music Koester first came to love had become known as "traditional" jazz to differentiate it from "bebop." "Bop" was the jazz of such young Turks as Charlie Parker and Dizzy Gillespie who began to record in the early to mid-1940s in the honking, rowdy, improvisational style that came to define the *Avant-garde* in jazz.

This struggle between "trad" and "bop" partisans, who insisted that their form of music was the one that defined properly the essence of jazz, and the other was either old and outdated (trad), or loud, obnoxious and merely derivative (bop), came to be called the Bop Wars. Though he was a partisan of trad jazz, Koester was also a fan of bop, and he always regarded the divisive tendencies as foolish, even as a teenager.

The radio was not the only source of jazz for a young man in Wichita in the 1940s. Koester was a regular in the record shops in the city, playing jazz records and buying as many as his limited resources allowed. He listened, at the same time, to blues artists such as Bessie Smith, since she was often backed by a jazz band that might include Louis Armstrong or Fletcher Henderson, but he did not buy them. In fact, he also heard some sides by Tampa Red and Memphis Minnie, but he basically ignored the vocals and guitars to listen to the horns. As a jazz fan, blues was best, for Koester, when it was most like jazz. Since blues was not on the radio he only heard it at the stores when he wanted to hear the band behind the featured performer.

One of Koester's favorite places was The Record Mart, owned by Irving Albert. Albert's store sold hillbilly, jazz, and blues and Koester says he got much of his education in the music there. Albert had built his fortune during the war-time recording ban by buying up a huge stash of old juke box records in Junction City, Texas, which included a considerable amount of blues. Albert made another fine deal when he met the used record dealer Mama Rols on a business trip to Chicago. She had warehouses full of used 78s, including a huge amount of hillbilly music that she couldn't sell; when they learned that Albert had warehouses full of Bluebird and Vocalion blues 78s that he couldn't sell, they made a swap that satisfied both of them.

It was not long, though, before the trad jazz fan came to love blues, too. "Blues is just a part of jazz," Koester says. "When I first started going out looking for blues records I didn't have a lot of money so I wouldn't buy the blues records right away. But I would play them at the record shop in Wichita. I later learned about second hand stores, where records were a hell of a lot cheaper, and juke box houses."

Besides the record stores and the radio Koester and his friends would also attempt to hear music in the saloons, but this was much trickier. Being under-age the owners of the saloons were wary of them and kept them out. When he would hang around outside one of the Wichita saloons in which a blues pianist played there was a guy who'd come out and say: "Don't hang around here, son."

Worse yet, when Koester and some high school buddies finally made their way in to one saloon to hear Lonnie Johnson (a couple of whose records Koester owned by then), they found themselves in trouble with the law for being in the black part of town. Koester arrived just as Johnson finished an electric violin tune and the Sheriff approached him and said: "These people don't want you in here, boy. You better come on out of there." Koester went down to the city jail and asked why they couldn't go to a "colored" club, and they just told him that the sheriff was from Oklahoma and he just has his ways. What can I say?

To compensate for this loss Koester caught Johnson in his hotel the next day on the phone and arranged to come interview him the following day at 3:30. Koester arrived a few minutes late and found that Johnson had already left. Johnson may have had the idea that this meeting was not going to do him any good, the sheriff being the way he was, and decided to split before anything nasty happened.

Koester says that he spent more time listening to records and sneaking into saloons than he did doing homework but he eventually made his way to St. Louis and St. Louis University in the later 1940s, where he spent the next four years studying film-making. When he graduated in 1952, however, it is obvious that he had been seduced by the music since he immediately became part-owner of a Dixieland jazz record store in St. Louis and left collecting of films as a hobby.

*

The Blue Note Record Shop was a second floor store on Delmar Avenue in St. Louis and the specialty was Dixieland jazz: Louis Armstrong, Jelly Roll Morton, Johnny Dodds, Bunk Johnson. Koester made a living owning the shop--but just barely. He would often close up the shop over the summer when sales were poor and go home to Wichita to live with his parents, who had rather dubious feelings concerning Bob's career choice, to say the least. But he kept at it. With the store only one year old, Koester decided to try a bit of recording on the side. His first issue set the pattern for his label--called Delmar Records after the street on which his store was located--and this pattern would remain the same for the next forty years.

In 1953 Koester heard a performance by a Dixieland group called the Windy City Six. He liked them very much and knew that they would not be recorded if it was up to the market-conscious major labels--bop or cool jazz, after all, was what the market demanded in 1953, not trad jazz. But to Koester this question of trends and fashions was irrelevant to the fact that the music was good so he decided he would record them. It was here that Delmar Records was born, conceived as a "bad" business decision based on loving the music and issuing a small run of good records for those who cared about it most.

Koester's first release was a burden on his Blue Note profits and he paid off the musicians in records. The record was not a great success financially but that was only a secondary consideration. The label, after all, was basically a hobby. Delmar Records could not exist alone and had to be funded by the profits from his retail business, a situation which would hold true to the present day. The label was really not meant to become his life's work--that it became so is still a bit of a surprise to Koester, since he ignored all the principles of "sound" business then as now.

Along with owning the record store and running his label, Koester was also a member of the St. Louis Jazz Club. This club was exactly what it sounds like: a group of trad jazz buffs who liked to get together and talk about and listen to jazz. This group decided, right around 1952 or 1953, to see if they could locate any of the old St. Louis jazz performers of the 1920s and 1930s. They consulted texts and noted recorded performances in which St. Louis streets and places were mentioned and then tried to figure out how to locate the performer who sang them.

How these jazz buffs came to find the musicians was rather ingenious: Charlie O'Brien was the cop who walked the beat that included Koester's store and Koester had come to know him a bit as a result. Koester knew that O'Brien was a good cop and that he had come to be interested in police work as a result of the fact that both of his parents had been murdered. He also knew that O'Brien liked older people, perhaps because of the early loss of his parents. When Koester broached the topic of using his investigative skills to find the musicians O'Brien was quite willing to help. He knew the black part of town and he had access to police files, which was often not a bad place to look for the whereabouts of the musicians. O'Brien was as good as they expected him to be and he located all of the old jazz musicians who were still living in St. Louis in the next couple of years.

Koester, of course, was not just a trad jazz buff, but had also come to be a blues buff. This was quite a different matter, however, as far as general recognition in America was concerned. The blues scene was much more isolated from the generality of white America than was jazz. Blues tended to live among Deep South blacks and in the black side of town and few middle class whites ever ventured to integrate their musical interests so far as to go listen to it, as Koester had attempted to do in Wichita. Though popular band leaders such as Duke Ellington or Count Basie may have performed sophisticated band versions of blues along with their jazz staples it was really only the female "classic" blues singers such as Bessie Smith and Alberta Hunter who came much to white attention and this was because of their relation to Louis Armstrong or Coleman Hawkins more than because of any great interest in blues.

The story of what happened in blues after the reign of the more sophisticated women performers of the early 1920s was known to most black Americans quite well: the arrival of the down-home bluesmen, the transition into a more pop and jazz-oriented blues in Chicago and New York in the 1930s; the rise of R & B in the Chicago ghetto. While this history was no news to black Americans in 1950, in a segregated society that discouraged contact between its black and white citizens this story was unknown to most of the whites. It was a subculture in the truest sense of the term: it existed under the surface of what most people would regard as "American culture" as a part of an excluded minority's segregated life.

The blues musician, himself, was a peripheral figure: whether it was Blind Willie McTell in Atlanta or Ramblin' Willard Thomas in Texas, the bluesman was almost universally a poor, and often itinerant, individual whose music was played in juke joints, country picnics or on the street. They were held in extreme contempt by the right-thinking (religious) element among blacks for playing the Devil's Music, and were invisible to whites.

It comes as no surprise, then, that to Koester in 1953 the blues world was both fascinating and quite exotic. This music, played by men who had been rural share-croppers, worked on levee gangs, hoboed around the country, or picked up musical tips from fellow prisoners in the infamous penitentiary farms such as Parchman Farm, was part of a way of life that was both an eye-opener and a shock. The fact that they produced this magnificent music, so gritty and close to the bone, was enough to make a liberal-minded white American wonder where they'd been all those years when this music was being produced.

The answer, of course, is that they were on the other side of town, across the tracks, or otherwise segregated from the black people who made the music as well as from their way of life. A working class Mississippi white man such as Jimmie Rodgers may have worked with blacks closely enough to have learned their music, but for the white middle classes this was not the case. Blues was played by people who were very alien to them, but also very close.

In 1953, as in 1963, there weren't many white Americans who really knew or cared about blues. There were probably even few black Americans who knew much about the blues musicians of the 1920s any more by the 1960s and there were almost no blues re-issues and no discography to tell us what had been recorded. To say that Koester was one in a million among white Americans in conceiving this enthusiasm for blues would be just about right.

CHAPTER X: BOB KOESTER, BIG JOE, AND SLEEPY JOHN

In the summer of 1958, Koester decided that St. Louis wasn't big enough for him and the fine bop shop that was his main competition and he decided, at the urgings of some friends, to go to Chicago. After some serious searching Koester found a store in July that he kept for only a year and then he bought Seymour's Record Mart, at 439 S. Wabash, in March 1959. Seymour's had been around since the 1940s and had a significant clientele already. There had been small concerts there in addition to the retail business and Koester would do the same in his own record stores.

One of the first things Koester did on arriving in Chicago was to call Studs Terkel to get Big Bill Broonzy's phone number. Terkel said that Broonzy was ill but gave him the number anyway. Broonzy's wife said that he was too ill to see anyone and he died a few days later. He missed seeing Broonzy, but Koester would meet, and record, many of the finest bluesmen of his day.

Just as he had done in St. Louis, Koester began to comb the blues bars and clubs on the South and West Sides as soon as he was established. Koester says that the West Side clubs were in rougher neighborhoods and the music was rougher, too. When he would see Magic Sam or Otis Rush--both of whom he would later record for Delmark--he noticed that they were more raucous than Muddy Waters was. He met Muddy pretty early on at Smitty's Corner, and Muddy would give him hints about other people to hear and record. Koester also went to I Spy on 63rd, Silvio's on Lake and Kedsi, and Curley's on W. Madison in these early days, and he heard some great blues from Elmore James, Howlin' Wolf and many others. There was never any hostility from either management or customers towards Koester or any white friends who might come to these bars, but the cops continued to stop him and search him with monotonous regularity and could not believe that any white man would really come to the black part of Chicago just to hear the music.

If cops harassed him residents were easy-going. They may not have loved having Koester and other whites in the clubs but their attitude is interestingly highlighted by the following anecdote: In the early 1960s, Koester recalls showing the British blues scholar Paul Oliver around Chicago and when they walked into Curley's on the South Side one Saturday night Oliver bumped by accident into another customer. Oliver said, in his very refined British accent, "Oh, I beg your pardon!" Koester says he sounded a bit like David Niven. The man he had bumped said: "Oh, you're British, aren't you? I thought you were white."

Koester continued for years to go the clubs every Saturday night while running Seymour's and Delmar all week, and the bars and clubs came to be a fertile source of music for Koester to record in the middle of the 1960s.

Yet, in the late 1950s and early 1960s, Koester was solely involved in recording the stars of the blues galaxy of the 1920s to 1940s, beginning with Speckled Red and Big Joe Williams in St. Louis, and continuing with Sleepy John Estes and Roosevelt Sykes in Chicago. After only a year and a half in Chicago, accordingly, Bob Koester came up with enough money to issue Delmar 602: *Piney Woods Blues*, by the Mississippi bluesman Big Joe Williams, and this was an important moment in his career.

*

When *Piney Woods* was issued in 1960 it sold 700 copies, which thrilled Koester. He never really thought that rough old blues such as Big Joe's would be popular enough to attract that sort of attention. He decided that the success of *Piney Woods* justified recording some more music with Joe, and when Joe showed up in Chicago in 1960, just after *Piney Woods* was released, Koester and he concluded a handshake deal. They recorded material enough for three albums a year and Koester said he'd only release one album a year. Joe agreed and promptly recorded three albums with Prestige, one with an indie, and a number of others over the next few years. Koester was angry at Joe for breaking contract with him, but since there was only a handshake he could not stop the others from releasing, and he liked Joe too much to stay angry with him. Koester never got enough of Joe.

Joe Williams (1903-1982) was a musician whose company young white guitarists and blues nuts sought eagerly in the 1960s. Though there were very few whites who even knew of the existence of this music at this point, those few who had discovered blues were often likely to seek out a guy like Joe for tips on how to play guitar and just to watch him play. Michael Bloomfield was one of these. Bloomfield came to be an important figure on the blues and popular music scene but when he first met Joe he was an unknown. Bloomfield is described in his 1980 memoir *Me and Big Joe* as "middle-aged, gifted, and white. Probably he is the foremost blues guitarist of his generation. From Bob Dylan, Paul Butterfield, and the Electric Flag in the Sixties to his own bands, records, and film soundtracks in the Seventies, music has felt his influence as performer, writer, arranger, and producer. In short, he has done a lot." Bloomfield was an early disciple of Big Joe's, a disciple who spent much time trying to learn what made Joe able to sing and play the way he did.

In *Me and Big Joe*, Bloomfield says of Joe: "[He] told me that Crawford, Mississippi, was his birthplace, and that since the early Thirties he'd done nothing but hobo around the country with his guitar. Now, most bluesmen I'd met had two jobs--they'd play and sing night times, but during the day they kept up a straight gig of one kind or another. But Big Joe never did that--he played and traveled, and that was it."

Koester says that Joe came and went from Chicago for years and they usually had no idea where he was. He would come around for a while and try to find a gig, or perhaps hit Koester up for $10, but he wasn't around for long. Koester calls Joe a "real roamin' rambler--the real thing. Not a great writer, but he knew every good song and he'd tell you where he got it. He even said that he'd stolen a part of 'Baby Please Don't Go' from a guy on Parchman Farm and he'd got another part from Mary Johnson."

When Koester moved to his third store in 1962, this time called Jazz Record Mart, around the corner at 7 W. Grand, Joe turned up and said he needed a place to live. Koester said that things at the moment were at a standstill. He'd been able to pay his rent in the new store but he could not issue any more Big Joe records, since he'd released two by then (*Blues on Highway 49* was the second, recorded in July 1961) and Joe had recorded promiscuously elsewhere. There were too many Big Joe albums on the market, and Koester was not able to give him work, but he said Joe could live in the basement of his store where there was a cot so long as the landlord didn't object. He gave Joe the keys to the store and he stayed there for some time.

Koester could not pay Joe much of anything for his occasional help in the store but he did have an arrangement with him. Since lots of white kids were beginning to come around looking for Joe, and Joe was playing informal sets constantly in the store, Koester would give Joe a dollar for each record the admiring audience bought in Jazz Record Mart. Just to make the sale a good one Joe would autograph the record.

Joe was very popular with a few blues nuts but that was not enough for him to make a living. In these years in Chicago he would be lucky to have one gig a week playing in some club and one every two weeks was more usual. Koester was involved in arranging gigs for bluesmen at a club called the Blind Pig and even though they managed to line up incredible talent it was hard to get a good audience. In conjunction with Michael Bloomfield, in 1960-61, Koester would line up the likes of Roosevelt Sykes, Little Brother Montgomery, Sunnyland Slim or Curtis Jones on piano, Ransom Knowling on bass, and Big Joe playing when he was around.

Though they had this great talent almost every week, the music was still so obscure to the general public that they could not even get the people in the Old Time School of Folk Music, who were in the same building, to come down and listen. "I was always pissed-off that I couldn't get these Old Time School people to come down--I even offered to let 'em in free the first time ..." To the Old Time people, though, blues meant Leadbelly and Big Bill, the two bluesmen who had become identified with "folk" music, and they were not interested in anyone else--certainly not in Big Joe Williams, who actually used an amplifier!

Joe stuck around for a while, at any rate, but he really was hard to deal with. Bloomfield describes his transformation from a kind, gentle man when he was sober, to a yelling, violent and threatening maniac when drunk. Koester had the same experiences of him. He and Joe would have horrible arguments and though Joe would be able to stop short of killing him, "he had that guitar up over his head at me a few times." Koester knew that this was Joe at age sixty and suspected that he had probably killed or maimed a few people in the rough days of his hobo life. The examples of rough bluesmen Leadbelly and Skip James indicate that this was quite likely.

By the time he was older, though, Koester thought that his temper and irresponsibility were not really a product of an evil streak, but of immaturity of nature. Joe would brag about getting a girl pregnant in Mississippi then abandoning her because he didn't want the responsibility of keeping a family by farming. "Joe would get pissed-off and leave town," Koester says, and this habit of running from his responsibilities was never to leave him. He'd let others pick up the pieces for him, instead.

Though the life of a rambling man sounds romantic, Koester says that a day in the life of Joe Williams was not too exciting. He had only a few gigs so he had to kill lots of time between them. Joe was illiterate, so he could not read to pass time and could not write down his own lyrics. And being illiterate meant that it was hard for him to find a regular job even if he'd wanted one. Joe did not work at Jazz Record Mart and Koester would give him money against the release of his next album. Joe would get up and brush his teeth behind the counter at the store then he'd play his guitar. He played and played which is why he was so good at it. The young white blues nuts would be able to hear Joe play informal sets so often because Joe had little else to do. He smoked, ate and drank far too much and he liked to watch cowboy movies on TV.

Meanwhile, in 1961 and 1962 Koester was to locate and record another blues legend of the 1930s: Sleepy John Estes. Estes would record five albums for Delmark that were released between 1962 and 1968, and Estes was one of the finest older blues artists to begin performing again in the 1960s "blues revival."

*

Somewhere in 1961 the Chicago film-maker David Blumenthal came into Seymour's and told Bob Koester about the following chain of events that led him to find Sleepy John Estes: Big Joe had told Memphis Slim that Estes was still alive in Brownsville; Memphis Slim had told Blumenthal about Estes and sent him to look for him; Big Joe told Koester that Estes was alive, but Koester was skeptical; Blumenthal went to see Estes and confirmed what Joe had told him.

(Koester's skepticism had been based on Big Bill's published assertion that Estes was in his eighties long ago and was now dead and this was where Koester learned how unreliable Broonzy's memory was.)

Koester listened to the soundtrack Blumenthal had made and was so impressed that he immediately began to correspond with Estes. In late 1961 or early 1962 Koester made his way down to Brownsville by train to meet Estes on his own turf. Koester had never been below the Mason-Dixon Line and he was appalled by the conditions there, as might be expected. There was constant hostility towards this white guy who was messing around among the blacks, and being in the middle of the Civil Rights Movement they no doubt thought Koester was there to make trouble for them. Koester went into a store in Brownsville that seemed mostly to sell mash for brewing beer and the old guy who was watching the store had some blues 78s in the back from the late 1940s. He was 78 years-old and had been a Wobbly so he was sympathetic to Koester's liberal politics and his disgust with the southern whites he'd met. The old man said it was hard to live around all these reactionaries!

When Koester finally came across Estes (who was about 57 at this time, contrary to Broonzy), he found him blind, as Blumenthal had said he was, and living in horrible poverty in a shack with his wife and a crowd of kids. Koester doesn't think he was even paying rent on the shack it was such a dump. He talked to Estes about coming back to Chicago to record an album and Estes agreed to do it. They looked up Estes' old partner, the harmonica master Hammie Nixon, and it was agreed that they would all go and cut an album as soon as possible.

The "as soon as possible" was necessary because of a problem that had developed: Koester had spent so much money on clothes and groceries for Estes and his family that he did not have enough money to pay for the return trip. He telegraphed back to the store and they told him that the weather was bad and they weren't making any money. Koester's employee went next store to Seymour's and got a loan from Morrie Davis, who owned a clothes store called the Davis Congress Shop, and sent this down to Koester.

With this money Koester and the others were able to make it to Fulton, Missouri where a friend of his at Westminster College set up a concert for John and Hammie. From the money they made in Fulton,

Koester was able to give them some pay and buy their tickets to Urbana-Champaign, where another friend had arranged a couple of concerts at the University of Illinois. After a trip to Purdue University for another gig they made their way to Chicago.

When they all arrived in Chicago something truly strange happened. Soon after arriving John said he'd like to go see his brother, who worked as a salesman at a place called the Davis Congress Shop. Koester knew the store, obviously, because it was the business right next to his own! It was very strange to learn that John's brother worked next door to his own store--and then to realize that the Sam Estes with whom he had been friendly for a couple years was John's brother. He only wished that he had made the connection earlier.

It was in March of 1962 that Koester recorded the music that would be issued on Delmar as *The Legend of Sleepy John Estes* (603) and *Brownsville Blues* (613). *Legend* features Estes on guitar and vocal, Hammie on harmonica, John "Knocky" Parker on piano, and Ed Wilkinson on bass. His renditions of "Someday Baby" and "Rats in My Kitchen" are excellent, and the lyrics are classics of the genre:

I don't care how long you go, I don't care how long you stay.
Someday baby you ain't gonna worry my mind any more.

Delivered in Estes' pained and earnest vocal, these lyrics become very poignant. He was still capable of offering up a bouncing dance tune like "Stop That Thing" in the same session but Estes' voice, one of the finest that the blues ever produced, was made for the blues more than for light-hearted juke tunes and his genius comes through best on songs such as "Someday Baby."

During their time together Koester learned quite a bit about Estes. He learned that Estes was called "Sleepy" by a record company because he had low blood pressure and could fall asleep on his feet. His poor diet and heavy drinking did not help matters most likely. Estes told Koester that he'd been blinded in one eye as a child when a stone was thrown at him. He'd been blinded in the other when he'd hoboed a ride on a sand car of a train coming to Chicago and a piece of sand had gotten into his eye.

Estes did not talk much and he was a very nice, peaceful, man. He was never violent or uncontrollable, even when drunk, and he was probably the victim of others' dishonesty because of his blindness and almost passive nature. The years of poverty had done nothing to elevate Estes' spirits and his own obviously sensitive and introspective nature, which is plain in his song writing, would make his misfortunes hard to bear.

After recording the music in March of 1962, Estes and Nixon stayed in Chicago for a while working whatever gigs they could find both in and out of the city. Koester was promoting some shows with Michael Bloomfield in 1963 at a teen nightclub on State Street called the Fickle Pickle and he had booked Jazz Gillum, Washboard Sam, Big Joe, and Muddy Waters Band at the same time he had found work there for John and Hammie. They played at the Fickle Pickle with the former Brownsville musician Yank Rachel, who now lived in Indianapolis and who had joined them for the music released on the second Sleepy John album. Koester remarked, as an indication of how much money there was in blues in the early 1960s, that the only time he ever made any money from the Fickle Pickle gigs was when Muddy Waters offered to play for $100. They made $101 in covers and Koester pocketed the buck--and this only because Muddy was a generous man.

In 1964 John recorded another session for Delmark which resulted in his second release, *Broke and Hungry* (608), featuring Hammie back on harmonica, Yank Rachel on mandolin, and Big Joe's buddy Michael Bloomfield on a couple of tracks playing guitar. It is another fine, rough, blues album that contributed to the growing popularity of Estes et al on the coffee house and college circuit and finally put some money in their pockets. And it was not long after the album was released that Koester would accompany Estes and Nixon to the Newport Folk Festival at which many white Americans first heard not only of Estes and Nixon, but of Mississippi John Hurt, Son House, Skip James, Robert Pete Williams, and others.

If playing Newport in 1964 was not enough Estes was off then to Europe with the American Folk Blues Festival of 1964, with Koester as his "lead boy." This giant tour featured Sonny Boy Williamson, Howlin' Wolf, Sunnyland Slim, Lightnin' Hopkins, Willie Dixon and Hubert Sumlin. They made the grand tour of Europe playing to large and enthusiastic audiences, recording concerts at television stations, and generally receiving the recognition, money, and respect they had not received enough of in the US.

Koester recalls that the tour really was not much fun. They would all get up early and go to the airport for their next gig. They'd wait for the baggage with nothing to do except making sure that all of the instruments had made it. Then they'd fly to their next destination, land, and wait an hour for the instruments. They'd take a bus to the hall for the sound check, go the hotel, eat, then wait around for the show to begin. They would then get back on the bus, go back to the hall, perform once or twice, and then back to the hotel once again. It was rather monotonous and the musicians would spend lots of time playing cards. Since it is a myth that bluesmen played better drunk there was also the necessity to keep the musicians sober before shows.

When the tour was over and all returned to the US things were about the same as before for John and Hammie: decent gigs, better money than they were used to, and lots of drinking. This continued for a few years and John recorded his last Delmark album in December, 1968. The album was a departure for John on record. He had recently wanted to record an album in a more contemporary style and when Koester learned that he had been sitting in with Hubert Sumlin, Sonny Boy Williamson and other more "modern" sounding blues musicians, he agreed to record an album on which John played amplified rhythm guitar and was accompanied by Sunnyland Slim on piano, Jimmy Dawkins on guitar, Odie Payne, Jr. on drums, Carey Bell on harmonica and Earl Hooker and Joe Harper splitting duties on bass. The resulting album, called *Electric Sleep* as a take-off on the Muddy Waters album *Electric Mud* of 1967, sold poorly but delighted Estes. The album was a fine example of a music that was no longer popular with black audiences, electric Chicago blues, but Estes was pleased to see that he could play with the younger guys even if no one bought the album.

One of the most trying aspects of working with Estes' partner Hammie Nixon in this period of "rediscovery" was that he was not all that bright. He was a great harmonica player but pretty slow otherwise. One of his problems was that he never could understand the concept of playing sets with a band. Koester saw Hammie sitting in with the Muddy Waters Band once and noticed that Hammie would never stop between songs. The band covered for him for most of the set and then Muddy went over and spoke patiently to Hammie for a minute and took the harmonica away from him. This prepared Koester for the problem during the recording of *Electric Sleep*, and they dealt with it just fine.

In the early 1970s, Koester made a deal to distribute Delmark in Japan, where there was great interest in Estes. They arranged for a Sleepy John Estes tour of Japan and for Trio Records to issue some Delmarks there. When John went to Japan he was a hit and he even seems to have had an album break the top 100 in Tokyo.

One might think that Estes' life would have changed for the better because of all this touring and recording, but that does not seem to have been the case. For one, Estes was popular--and often did encores on the European tour--but white blues enthusiasts had a tendency to idolize the guitar players to the detriment of the great vocalists and John was a good guitarist but not a great one. It was the vocal, the part of blues that is most unique and inimitable, that was Estes' forte and this was not enough to make him as much money as some of the other blues musicians who were "rediscovered" in the blues revival. His roughness and grittiness also made him a less likely candidate for a major label and Delmark was a small market label. He sold records for Delmark, so some whites were listening to the vocal rather than just the guitar, but not enough to land Estes a big deal.

Estes' life changed but it was never what it should have been. "His demeanor changed in Europe," Koester says. "In the States I kinda got the impression from Hammie that they felt they were kinda conning us, you know, with this old country music that they'd lived with all their lives." In Europe the respect seemed to make him prouder and more confident. But the money Estes made never seemed to last. Koester kept some of the money from Europe back from Estes and gave it to him later, since his money in Europe disappeared well before it could do him any good.

It was, unfortunately, the same in the US: they would make some money from touring or recording then go back to Brownsville and "there'd be a massive amount of drinking, during which the money seemed to disappear." When Koester received the checks from Trio Records for John's Japanese successes he sent not only Estes' part of the check but all of it so that John would have the money while he lived. "He may still be over-drawn but I don't really care," he says. Estes lived in a HUD house for a while in the 1970s but even though he was receiving all of the profits from the Japanese tour and recordings the payments soon ceased and he had to move. Koester has no idea where this money was going, but suspects that someone was ripping Estes off. When Estes died in 1977 he was still in poverty but not broke and hungry, at least.

CHAPTER XI: BOB KOESTER, JUNIOR WELLS, AND MAGIC SAM

Sometime in 1963, Bob Koester got a phone call from a college kid in Atlanta named George Mitchell. Mitchell said that he'd heard Big Joe's *Piney Woods Blues* on Delmar and he asked Koester if he could work for him. Mitchell had no idea how much Delmar depended on Jazz Record Mart for its existence and Koester said he couldn't afford to pay anyone to work for him. Before they got off the phone, Koester told Mitchell to look him up if he was ever in town and said good bye.

Mitchell was on the next bus to Chicago. When he arrived at Koester's door, Koester was very amused and "hired him for pathetic money--I think he actually stayed at my pad for a while because I couldn't pay him enough money to live in a rooming house." Mitchell later roomed with a few other guys who hung around Jazz Record Mart and most of his time with Koester was devoted to working in the store: putting prices on albums, working the register, etc.

Mitchell's clean-cut, upper middle class, Druid Hills appearance was deceptive, of course. He may have dressed like a prep school boy, but he and a friend in Atlanta, Roger Brown, were hard core blues enthusiasts and they had sought out many of the surviving blues greats in Memphis. They were serious about blues, much wilder than they looked, and George wanted to see if he could make a living working around the music while Roger stayed at Emory University hitting the books.

While George was working at Jazz Record Mart, it happened that Big Joe was living in the basement. George came to know Joe pretty well and heard many of his impromptu sets over the next year. Joe, Bob and George had a regular dinner of Southern fried chicken that Joe prepared on Wednesday nights and Koester says that Joe had a way of frying the chicken such that the grease was not on the food but was on everything else in the vicinity of the kitchen.

George spent lots of time combing the clubs with Joe and Mike Bloomfield following Joe's hints about who to hear and where to find them. George and Bloomfield even made a trip to St. Louis with Joe scouting talent for Delmar. Bloomfield's *Me and Big Joe* describes their reaction to the heavy drinking (which made the two younger men very ill but only left Joe rowdy and cantankerous), the unaccustomed surroundings of slum living, and the unaccustomed harshness of Joe's rambling ways. Joe's way of life, in fact, left both of them gasping for breath. Bloomfield had to admit that he couldn't imitate Joe's blues, even after a huge effort, because this unaccustomed place in the slums was where Joe's blues really lived, and that Bloomfield could not live there.

St. Louis was not Mitchell's only trip to look for bluesmen at this time. He went on trips to find Buddy Moss in his home town of Atlanta and Kokomo Arnold in Memphis. Buddy Moss, a part of the Atlanta scene in the 1930s before going to prison for murdering his wife in 1935, was a man whose legendary bad temper had not bettered over the years, even if his playing had. George made some demos in Moss's living room, intending to see if he could land Moss a recording contract (the demos begin with Moss saying: "I dedicate this song to Bob Koester of Delmar Records"), and thought that Moss was going to sign on. The demos are beautiful examples of Piedmont blues, and Koester was, in fact, quite impressed.

Bob Koester says that negotiations for a contract broke down when Moss demanded that he be recorded with a full band of guitar, bass, drums, and horn, while Koester could only afford maybe drums or bass, preferably solo. As well-known as Delmar was among blues enthusiasts, Koester was not a wealthy man, and he could not afford to put all of his resources into paying for a band with Buddy. He was forced to break off the negotiations then and there.

George was no more successful with Kokomo Arnold, the frenetic guitarist whose "Paddlin' Madeline Blues" of 1930 was one of the most distinctive guitar pieces ever recorded and whose "Milk Cow Blues" of 1934 was covered by Robert Johnson —and even by Elvis Presley and Eddie Cochran. Mitchell managed to locate Arnold at his Memphis home, but he discovered that Arnold was completely uninterested in recording, made plenty of money selling moonshine, and was only interested in music to the extent that he liked to play rock and roll tunes for his granddaughter. Mitchell tried to convince him to come to Chicago and record but Arnold wouldn't budge and Mitchell left without achieving his goal.

But Mitchell did put Koester on to some new talent in Chicago and helped Koester expand into recording musicians at home. Mitchell had caught Junior Wells playing at Theresa's on the West Side one night and he told Koester about him as soon as possible. Wells had been born in Memphis in 1934 and had moved with his mother to Chicago in 1946. He had begun to play harmonica in Memphis and was sneaking into clubs in Chicago to sit in with the likes of Tampa Red and Sunnyland Slim beginning in 1948. He soon began to sit in with the Muddy Waters Band and when Little Walter left he took his place in the band. Junior cut some singles for the States label around this time but was soon inducted into the army-- one of his States sessions was actually cut while he was AWOL.

Though Junior had cut some 45s, it was not until 1964 that George told Koester about him. Koester soon located Wells and convinced him to record an album and the result was a Chicago blues classic, *Hoodoo Man Blues* (612), recorded in 1965 with a young Buddy Guy on guitar. As Koester says on the album notes: "*Hoodoo Man Blues* is not only Junior Wells' initial LP appearance, it is damn near the first LP by a Chicago blues band." While Chess and some other labels had reissued some 45s by Muddy, Sonny Boy and others, they had not attempted to produce a unified set of music rather than a collection of juke box hits like *The Best of Muddy Waters*. Koester's idea was to record a set that was much like what the band would play in their club sessions and *Hoodoo Man* captures this feel beautifully.

Wells is not only an excellent harmonica player, but a soulful and passionate vocalist. A song such as "In the Wee Hours" seems to have soul or gospel influence in the vocal, which sets it apart even from other songs on the album, but there is not a clunker in the set. Even their version of Lieber and Stoller's "Hound Dog" has considerable merit. *Hoodoo Man* both launched Junior Well's career as a major blues artist and became Delmark's biggest selling album, selling 1500 copies the first year.

With the success of Wells' album, Koester decided that he would try another of the locals who had no contract with a major label and this eventually led him to the blues and soul of Samuel Maghett, who performed around the clubs under the name Magic Sam. Maghett was born in Mississippi in 1937 and moved to Chicago in 1950. He played only guitar at first, not wanting to sing because of shyness, but he was encouraged to sing as well as play by some friends and he honed his vocal style in a gospel group.

The time he spent singing gospel gave Sam's vocal the soul sound that he used to such advantage singing his blues and soul in Chicago in the later 1950s and 1960s. Sam made some sides for the Cobra label in 1957, a few for Chief in 1960 and 1961, and then some for the Crash label in 1966, before coming to the studio to cut a Delmark classic of Chicago blues and soul, *West Side Soul* (615) of 1967. *West Side Soul* was cut in the same manner as *Hoodoo Man* had been: the band, which included Mighty Joe Young on guitar, played a set as they would play it in the clubs and the result is a tight set of blues and soul tunes that were not just a collection of hits, but a set that had worked well in live performance. This album topped Junior Wells' as Delmark's best seller, and though Koester was very worried about recording so unorthodox a bluesman as Sam was, he was never in doubt about how good the music was. Soul was the music of choice among most of the younger blacks even by the later 1950s, so recording blues in 1967 was mostly for the white market, as well as older blacks. The combination of blues and soul in Magic Sam was an appropriate combination of genres for its time and it stands as a classic album because it expresses so well a period in Chicago's musical history.

During this time, Bob Koester not only recorded Junior and Sam, but also sought out Roosevelt Sykes, Arthur "Big Boy" Crudup, and J.B. Hutto. J. B. Hutto was a boisterous, rowdy, slide guitarist born in 1926 in Augusta, Georgia. Hutto had moved with his family to Chicago in 1941 so that his father could find work in the mills. The family lived on the rough West Side and Hutto took up drums at the age of twenty, though he decided that he really wanted to play guitar a couple of years later after hearing Big Bill play. Hutto formed the Hawks in 1948 and soon moved to the South Side with his wife, playing at Turner's for the next ten years. When Koester caught up to Hutto in 1966 to record for Delmark, they worked for the next couple of years trying to get together enough material for an album, and the result was the blues party stomp *Hawk Squat* (617) of 1968. With the Hawks and Sunnyland Slim (who mostly played organ) present on the sessions, the music is fast and loud, and Hutto's debt to Elmore James and

Robert Nighthawk is evident throughout. The album also features Hutto's strong vocals soaring over the band's efforts, and though he was not as subtle as were Wells and Maghett, he was a compelling vocalist whose singing is probably underrated in comparison to his guitar playing. Hutto cut a couple more Delmark albums (618 and 636) before dying in 1983.

Koester located Arthur Crudup, whom he had heard was still alive and had recorded in 1959, by the tried and true method of sending him a letter care of the postmaster in one of the Mississippi towns he mentioned in a song he'd recorded. Crudup responded from a town in Virginia and he was brought to Chicago in 1967 to record his first Delmark album.

Crudup's story is already well known. Born in Mississippi in 1901, he was discovered playing on the Chicago streets in 1941 by Lester Melrose of RCA Records' Bluebird label. Crudup recorded a series of blues tunes in a unique style that sounds neither like down-home blues nor like the R & B of other Chicago musicians of his day. His "Mean Old Frisco Blues" of 1942, with Ransom Knowling on bass, and "That's All Right Mama" of 1946, with Melvin Draper on drums, are concerned much more with rhythm than they are with guitar virtuosity, and Crudup's high-pitched vocal gives a peculiarly pensive quality to his recordings. Elvis Presley, of course, covered "That's All Right" very closely for his first single on Sun Records in Memphis in 1954, following it with a version of Kokomo Arnold's "Milk Cow Blues," and since Crudup had signed away the rights to the song, he got not a cent for Presley's use of it.

Tired of being ripped off by record companies, Crudup recorded under a variety of names in the 1950s to make some money. Crudup liked Koester, who was always fair and up-front with his artists, though he couldn't pay them much. Delmark 621 was issued with music from the 1968 and 1969 sessions that Crudup recorded with Willie Dixon and Ransom Knowling, respectively, on bass, and the album features Crudup's trademark high-pitched, almost falsetto vocal over his intricately syncopated guitar playing. Crudup was very shy his whole life, so he really did not have a performing set like Junior Wells or J.B. Hutto, and the album is made up of mellow, informal songs that fit together nicely because they sound so much like a back porch set Crudup might play for a few friends. Most of the album is original material with an interesting version of John Lee Hooker's "I'm In the Mood" included as well.

It was in 1970 that Delmark recorded *Feel Like Blowing My Horn* (632) by Roosevelt Sykes. Sykes (b. 1906) is too well known to require introduction--he is usually considered the founder of blues piano style and he had already recorded for Delmark in 1962 and after. *Feel Like Blowing My Horn* has the New Orleans-tinged sound that he had learned growing up in that city, and Sykes was always a favorite of the Dixieland jazz fan Koester.

For this session with Sykes, Koester wanted to hire the noted side man Robert Jr. Lockwood to play guitar. Lockwood had moved to Cleveland in 1961, and when Koester contacted him he refused to accompany Sykes unless he could record an album of his own while he was there. The result was that Sykes recorded his album on a Monday and Tuesday in August of 1970, and on Wednesday and Thursday Lockwood recorded his first album as a band leader, *Steady Rolling Man* (630), with veteran session men Louis and Dave Meyers on guitar and bass and Fred Below on drums. The Lockwood album demonstrates that Lockwood was, in essence, more of a session man than a leader, and the songs have a certain quality of going through the motions about them, as do his later solo projects. Lockwood seems to have been at his best feeding off the talent of others, as his Candid sessions with Otis Spann demonstrate very well.

Another impressive session from this period is the first Delmark album of the harmonica player Carey Bell, *Carey Bell's Blues Harp* (622). Bell had been discovered by the white harmonica player Charlie Musselwhite playing in small West Side clubs. Musselwhite, who had worked for Koester briefly in the early 1960s at Jazz Record Mart (parting from this job in the wake of throwing an ashtray at Koester and punching him in the face after a disagreement concerning some signs Musselwhite was making), recommended that Koester record Bell and Koester readily agreed. Bell made his Delmark album of 1969 with the band that he usually worked with in the clubs: Jimmy "Fastfingers" Dawkins on guitar, Pinetop Perkins on piano, Joe Harper on bass and W. Walker on drums. The album features covers of Little Walter tunes, Willie Dixon's "I'm Ready," as well as half a dozen of Bell's originals, and it follows the usual Delmark method of approximating the band's club sets. Bell is an excellent harmonica player and a good vocalist and the support of Jimmy Dawkins' quick and delicate guitar work and Pinetop Perkins on the piano is especially worthy of note.

In the 1970s to 1990s, Koester would record old-timers Little Brother Montgomery, Edith Wilson, Floyd McDaniel and Golden "Big" Wheeler in addition to younger artists such as current best-seller Otis Rush and Eddy Clearwater. In addition to recording new music Delmark has also expanded into another arena: it was in the later 1970s and 1980s that Koester began to purchase masters from other companies. Masters from Apollo Records have provided Koester with some splendid sessions of the blues pianist Sunnyland Slim from 1949, issued as *House Rent Party* (655); short-lived Parkway Records, which had been sold very soon after coming into existence to Fred Mendelsohn of Regal Records, provided Koester some early sides of the blues harp player Little Walter, guitarist J.B. Lenoir and more of Sunnyland Slim, issued as *The Blues World of Little Walter* (648); Pearl Records brought some rollicking R & B sides by the slide guitarist Robert Nighthawk from 1951, *Rocks In My Pillow* (P 11).

The masters to some fine sessions of the New Orleans jazz artist Sun Ra, with a virtual cult following, have also been helpful to Delmark, as has the purchase of some informal sessions recorded of lesser known Chicago blues musicians by Ralph Bass, who had given T-Bone Walker and James Brown their breaks, in 1977.

*

Though he recorded much music that was very familiar to him from his club crawling and record collecting, Koester was not simply recording his own favorites--"I record what I damn please," as he puts it, and this includes recording something *Avant garde* that is not really even that close to his heart. In the later 1960s, this trad jazz and blues enthusiast chose to record, with the encouragement of some local writers, the Chicago-based Association for the Advancement of Creative Music (AACM), a group of jazz musicians who were playing in a form of collective improvisation that was radically experimental and dissonant in approach. As he says in the liner notes to the CD *Delmark 40th Anniversary: Jazz*: "I didn't understand what the

AACM was doing, but I knew the only chance I had to make some really great records would be something like this. I felt these guys were really important to the history of jazz."

In the case of the AACM, Koester knew that they would be a financial drag, but also that there is more to music than doing what sells. His Jazz Record Mart on 7 W. Grand was doing okay business, and he was able to dump JRM money into Delmark to support the music. He moved JRM to a bigger store on N. Lincoln in 1970 and he ran Delmark out of a couple of desks in a back room.

With the continued success of the blues catalog, Delmark was able to continue to record the AACM into the 1970s, and Koester regards this aspect of Delmark's success as more significant than their success with blues. As he sees it, the blues material might have found its way onto disc without him, eventually, but the AACM was simply too far outside popular tastes, too *Avant garde*, to be considered by those who are just trying to make a buck at all costs. In the early days of his label, Koester recalls, "I always figured the jazz records would make the money and the blues records would be, you know, a good cause, a noble experiment or something. It's turned out pretty much the other way around!"

The new JRM on Lincoln Avenue was a bigger store than the one at 7 W. Grand, but when you look at it today it's still amazing that this modest little store with a hand painted sign would be so significant to jazz and blues buffs in the US, Western Europe and Japan for whom Delmark was a significant player in the music world. The store inside has the bar from an old saloon as its counter and the walls were lined with browser boxes full of LPs, boxes of sale albums, 99 cent singles, and so on. Today, this space is used for storage, mostly, and the boxes of singles and left-over sale bins are probably bound for the dumpster. But the place is much in the Delmark and JRM spirit: pretty small, a bit untidy, not at all "square business" (as Koester refers to the corporate world), but a place where you can get your hands on great jazz and blues.

Koester moved from Lincoln Avenue back next door to his old store at 7 W. Grand in 1981--it was now Jazz Record Mart at 11 W. Grand and they would stay there until the summer of 1995. There is a yuppie bar and grill on the spot of both his old W. Grand stores today and he can walk you through and show you where the cash register was, where the browser boxes were for the LPs and the CDs, the sale bins, the storage room, the back alley where they had a few concerts before complaints about noise put an end to them. The alley is now closed in and leads to the kitchen. The warehouse now has pool tables. The place where the sale LPs were is now just an area next to some booths. There is another floor added to house a microbrewery. And Koester pointed out to the waitress that the bricks had looked better in his day since they were now glazed and had lost their redness.

She had no opinion on the matter.

It is only in 1995 that the scene changes to the extent that Delmark and Jazz Record Mart have separate offices. The Delmark offices in Lincoln Park are now much more than a number of desks in a back room though they are no more pretentious than they ever were. Jazz Record Mart, the largest jazz record store in the world, is now around the corner from 11 W. at 444 S. Wabash. The bigger, snazzier JRM now shares quarters with a CPA, an advertising agency, and something called an image bank.

Koester's brother laughs at what he calls Bob's "yuppie store" on S. Wabash, but the new quarters and more mall-like appearance have not changed the place in its essence: you go in and find the CD browser bins in the front; many bins of used LPs with lots of customers flipping through them in the back of the store; sale bins with 99 cent LPs; a little place roped off for a band to play; and a space that is being prepared for the book department, a new experiment for Koester. The atmosphere is informal and relaxed, and Koester even has volunteers working in the store--people who like the music and the atmosphere so much that they give up their Saturdays to come in and price LPs. Koester gives them a hefty break on purchases, of course, but try to imagine a volunteer down at your local strip mall record shop? Not even within the realm of possibility.

One of the defining images of Bob Koester's approach to his business is that you can find him down at Jazz Record Mart on a Saturday afternoon doing what he has done for forty years: sitting in front of a pile of used jazz LPs, looking at them for scratches, cleaning them off with a cloth if needed, and putting the appropriate price on the record jacket. He mostly just plops a "$3.99" or "$6.99" on them without comment, but every once in a while he will whistle or say "whoa!" and show you an original Miles Davis LP from Blue Note which will be put to one side and processed later.

    Koester need not come down to 444 S. Wabash to price used records: he does it because likes it. He's had offers from the majors to buy his label and work for them which would make him much more money and put him into the nest of corporate luxury of which most Americans dream. But Bob Koester just isn't interested. He belongs to the National Association of Independent Record Distributors (NAIRD), along with such labels as Alligator, Arhoolie, and Flying Fish Records, and these "music labels," as he calls them to differentiate them from the corporate labels, try to do business well enough to keep the music in circulation but won't get so "square business" that their own music would no longer suffice. "If you get too square business--if you run it like a normal business--you're in trouble."

    Koester says that the majors will only market a big seller and then let it go out of print the moment it no longer brings in a certain level of sales. "If I were to merge with a major label the first thing they'd do is delete half the catalog. And a year later they'd delete another third. And a lot of those are good records that just don't happen to sell well. I've got no patience with that kinda bullshit. I do not want to be involved with that." It is for this reason that Koester stays so active in the running and promotion of JRM. The bigger the store is the more he can sink into Delmark free of the necessity to make decisions based merely on the bottom line.

    Love of the music, on the other hand, is hardly a part of corporate music. "I do see the business being taken over by the number-crunchers and the lawyers, and man, I mean, if they can figure it out-- well, good luck, man! I don't think they will!"

    Koester is justifiably proud of all that he has accomplished with both JRM and Delmark. If you ask him if he wants to get bigger, he gets a bit pissed off as witness the following exchange:

    Me: "Do you ever think about trying to get bigger, or do you kinda think that would just fuck things up?"

    Koester: "I got bigger, man! I'm a whole lot bigger! You just got the Cooks tour of 7 and 11 W. Grand--we're a whole lot bigger here! I don't want to be corporate--I don't want a boss. The whole idea...Being in business for yourself you don't have a boss. Your boss is the rent man. Your boss is the creditor. And if you watch your ass, they don't give you too much grief...I'm very interested in my independence and if I went broke as a label and had to stop doing it I'd just run the store. If the store went broke I'd just run the label, if I had it. If both of them went broke I'd sell movies. I don't think 'bigness.'"

Koester won't do his business out of the board room partly because he doesn't think that jazz lives there very well. "I value my independence considerably and jazz has to be independent!" In reference to the major labels' attempts to produce music so inoffensive that it might appeal to any segment of society, he laughs: "You can sell some of the people some of the time; and some of the people all of the time; but you can't sell all of the people all of the time. And that's what the majors are trying to do." The majors will record John Lee Hooker but only if he is surrounded by rock stars who only play a little or no blues. As a result, the music is among the worst the artists have ever recorded but sells more than their best by a long shot.

This is where the independent labels, such as Delmark, come into play. They record the best music they can find without the necessity that it be a million seller. Sleepy John Estes, Magic Sam and Big Joe Williams sell some records but the music is too genuine, too close to where the blues really live, to appeal to that many people--and this is okay with Bob Koester. At the majors, Koester says, he would produce music that not that many people would like so he'd be out on the street again soon, anyway. "I'd have to deal with people who don't understand the music. There are enough bad blues being made without me adding to it."

So, Bob Koester would rather continue to make good blues and jazz in Chicago ("Movin' it to Hollywood ain't gonna help") than make a mint in LA or New York. He'd rather price used LPs on Saturdays than be at a board meeting. He'd rather drive a Subaru wagon than do what it takes to drive a Mercedes. He's had his chances to go corporate but just had no interest. Koester is independent, successful, and reports to no boss or bosses. They lose some money now and again at Delmark, but Jazz Record Mart is doing well. He has been at it for forty-two years now and sometimes his plans don't work out too well for one reason or another. He admits that some of the music he's recorded is just no good and he'd like to bury the masters at sea, but he is proud of the fact that Delmark had made so much that is simply great.

Delmark is a small business in an era of conglomerates and corporate take-over, and it is because his market is people who love the music that Bob Koester is able to stay in business. Delmark may lose money on some of their projects, "But we still have the master, and there's always tomorrow to sell 'em. And that's good enough for me." That about sums up Koester's approach and the personality of Delmark Records.

CHAPTER XII: AN INTERVIEW WITH SAMUEL B. CHARTERS (4/28/1996)

CHARTERS: I was born in 1929 and my mother's older brother had a jazz orchestra, which had been playing together since 1925. They were deeply interested and excited by jazz. My father, when my mother met him, he was playing banjo--they were upper class, private school preppies--they found it exciting so they could afford to play jazz. So, I was born into rehearsals in the large living room and jazz recordings. My mother's younger sister...in 1930, when I was about a year old, married a trumpet player who'd come out of Texas with the Teagarten brothers and he was on tour with the Ben Burney Orchestra. So he would drift through. And there were times that I would find Jack Teagarten hung up by his coat collar in the hall closet. The visiting band members would drift through. I remember one time my two uncles disappeared off to New York and hitchhiked back because he wanted to see the new trumpet player in the Duke Ellington Orchestra. And I remember [this uncle] fell definitely in love with a girl and I remember he took to play for her Bessie Smith's "Nobody Knows You When You're Down and Out" hoping this would impress her. It has a wonderful humming chorus--Bessie hums the second verse--and the girl listened to this record very uncomfortably and finally at the end she said, "She sure can hum!"

In a way I'm unusual in that I grew up in a complete jazz background in which my younger brother...he was a mascot to Ray McKinley the drummer who had come out of New Orleans, and he was in with the Bob Crosby Orchestra where he acted as band boy. He was having a long correspondence with Ray McKinley, who was trying to get him off the wild excitement for jazz--make sure he didn't mess his life up. So, I grew up in a world of band rehearsals, blues records, and a whole consciousness of jazz--I'm not saying [that this was all]. The family also played ragtime, also played Debussy, also was involved in hearing Bartok's new music. It was a general musical cultural interest in which jazz was central.

It's interesting to me that when I was a baby, one or two years old, I was taken to hear the band rehearse in the large hotel dance hall where they played--the Hotel Webster in Pittsburgh near the

University of Pittsburgh campus--and that hall had a classic 20s sound. It was largely wooden, there were high ceilings, and there was incredible warm echo. When I listen to my 78s from the 20s occasionally I can hear this. The Jean Goldkette Orchestra recorded in a room like this, some of the Ellington sessions were done in a room like this, and it brings me back right to my childhood being held in my mother's arms hearing a jazz orchestra from 1930 playing in one of these wonderful, resonant, warm halls. So, I never had any idea that I was--I thought everyone had this background!

So, when we moved to California when I was a teenager--fifteen years old we moved to Sacramento--suddenly I was completely without any support! I grew up with it and here nobody even knew about it. So I immediately began in high school--they would ask me to write something and I would write about Bix Beiderbecke. I did radio programs since I was sixteen years old. And I was leading--playing clarinet, playing jazz steadily all this time; I had my first orchestra when I was thirteen; I was playing all the time, playing jazz. I was not very good. I had no natural abilities, but I soldiered on, and it was this that directly lead me to the beginning of the research.

I went to New Orleans--my father was a switchman for the railroad--and he could get me a pass. So, I would sit in the day coach, in 1950--December 1950--to New Orleans, and I was going to take clarinet lessons from George Lewis, who at that point was barely known except for those AM recordings that Bill Russell had done. So, I got off this train at Union Station without knowing anything (just a kid) and I walked out and took a street car down St. Charles Ave., found a flop house which didn't even have walls--it just had wooden partitions and chicken wire. I checked in there and had my clarinet and my little bag and then I walked out across Canal Street, up Bourbon (which was very quiet in those days), and there was a club called the Paddock Lounge and there was a band playing. I walked in and there was Bill Matthews Band with all those wonderful guys: Ernie Caglietti on trumpet and Alfred Burbank on clarinet. And I just stood there stunned and went up to them during the break and said could they give me George Lewis's number. Immediately, just absolutely no problem at all--everyone was close friends--I just sat around and idolized them. So, I began the next week to take clarinet lessons with George, who lived up on St. Philip St. I don't know if you know about George, but he was a legend to us all. He was a living presence who was also a wonderfully gentle and decent guy. He had no electricity. We would sit there by a kerosene lamp in his kitchen and do a two clarinet duet. I'd play the melody and he would show me all the variations. He'd go on and play 15 or 20 choruses and show me--in a gentle way--all of the things I would never have thought of on my own!

And then one night--and this is where it all begins--late one afternoon I was walking through the French Quarter and I saw George and Jim Robinson, his trombone player, and they were all dressed up at 4:30 on a Sunday afternoon and I said why are you all dressed up? They said they'd been to a funeral. Who'd died, I said politely, and they said it was one of the great trumpet players named Big Bama. And I was stunned because at that point I had read every book on jazz, I had read every article I knew of on jazz, and certainly, I had never heard of Big Bama. So, the next day George--he worked as a stevedore, so he had to take little naps in the evening before he would go out and play--because it was very hard! A 5'3", 130 pound stevedore--a spindly little guy. He would let me come during his nap and sit and talk and I came the next day and sat at the foot of the bed and said, "Tell me about Big Bama." And George began talking about jazz in New Orleans and all the men I'd never heard of all the names and all the musicians, and right then, it immediately started at that point. When I moved to New Orleans, my first book was the biographical dictionary, first published in 1958, after all those years of interviews, going all over finding people.

So, I did my Army, came out of the Army, was in and out of New Orleans during that time, then moved there in '54. And I remember that I was walking along and seeing a broken record outside the old furniture store and seeing that it was a Bessie Smith. I'm thinking, "Oh, my God," and realizing that the blues was such a crucial part of all this--even though, with our jazz orientation--but as I say, the blues was so deep within the black community that even those of us who were at the edges weren't getting it. We just didn't know. There were those two records that I listened to in 1948, there was a band I was playing with in Berkeley, and we had the Blind Willie Johnson "Dark

Is the Night" and we had the acetate copy of the Robert Johnson "Stones In My Passway." We would listen to one, one night, then the next night the other, after we'd finished rehearsing.

M. ISMAIL: So it wasn't all Bessie Smith and Ida Cox and people like that--you actually also knew about those other guys.

CHARTERS: This is it, and as I say it began in the 40s. In '53 I first tried to look for Robert Johnson because I'd understood--I'd read those quotings on the masters and they said they'd been recorded in San Antonio. So, I just went to San Antonio. And also, at the same time, I'd bought a tape recorder and I began doing research looking for Blind Willie Johnson and that became my first major recording project: going over Texas with my old Petron green-eyed monster recording people who led me on the search for Blind Willie. That became my first real Folkways production when it was finally released four years later.

The next easy, direct, connection was that we'd heard that the Memphis Jug Band was still playing in Memphis in '56. So, I went up to Fred Ramsey (I'd met him in '54 in New Orleans when he was on a Guggenheim recording in Alabama, essentially redoing Harold Courlander's work in Livingston County, which I didn't know)--but there was Fred telling me how you do this, and what you did, and how you kept track of your notes, and record everything, and I had my tape recorder and all of this music--and that's how I began. I did the Mobile Strugglers, a country skiffle band--I did that in May of '54-- and did all the Blind Willie recording and was doing a lot of New Orleans recording too, but we were all discovering that New Orleans music was only the beginning. New Orleans was in many ways not the best place to start because New Orleans had almost no blues tradition. There was one singer, named Black Walter Nelson, who played some electric blues in the clubs, so we all knew him, but we also knew that he wasn't stunning. At the same time that I was going through Texas I was hoping to find Lightnin' Hopkins because we all listened to black radio and we were hearing a lot of rhythm and blues and the one who really took us back to Blind Willie Johnson and Robert Johnson was Lightnin' Hopkins. He was the only thing we were hearing on the radio that was unaccompanied blues guitar and we didn't know how to find him. Then it turned out that he had a cousin who was cooking at the Bourbon House, sort've a run-down place on Bourbon Street where we all ate dinner.

MI: So you thought Lightnin' Hopkins might be in New Orleans?

CHARTERS: Well, no, I knew he was in Texas and I'd go through Texas looking for these--first, I was only looking for Robert Johnson during my first Texas swing, then did quite an extensive search for Blind Willie Johnson. I was in Berkeley and I was in New Orleans, I was going back and forth, back and forth, and Texas was in the middle. So, the next group of searches were for Lightnin' trying to find him in the beginning of the mid '50s.

MI: Blind Willie Johnson died somewhere in the late 40's--or 30's--didn't he?

CHARTERS: Well, it turns out, just after I wrote this set of notes I'd won an award for, this kid in Texas said "Oh, by the way, I've just found Blind Willie's death certificate--after doing an enormous amount of work we now have Blind Willie's story straight--he died around '44 or '45, I can't remember exactly when. I'd thought it was 1948. It was '53 when I found the widow, Angeline.

MI: And so, in the process of looking for him did you record other people?

CHARTERS: I recorded people who would have known him--if you've ever heard this record, it's a series of people talking about Blind Willie, singing songs that he knew, and then putting a narrative of the search to find him. Everyone was blind, everyone was religious. On the back side of the record I put re-issues and my theme at this point was how young farm hands who were blind, how the hell they lived. So on the back side of the record I put, I think, five tracks of Blind Willie Johnson. I also put Blind Lemon Jefferson, Blind Willie McTell--I was already re-issuing country blues in 1954.

In 1956, at Fred Ramsey's insistence, I brought these tapes up to Moe Asch's Folkways in a cardboard box in an old car. Moe said "Leave 'em," and then the next day he said "Okay, I'll put 'em out." So, I drove back to New Orleans and went through Memphis, on the way back in the Fall of '56--I guess it would've been early December--and by God, there was the Memphis Jug Band, and Gus Cannon, and--[laughs with pleasure]--I had an incredible time. The rest of the recordings came out on *American Skiffle Bands* in 1956. By then I was deeply involved--deeply immersed--and I was gathering material on all the blues singers, but my New Orleans research was taking 90% of my time. But there was 10% I could do on the blues, so I was always asking about any blues singers. But as I say, Louisiana was not the most fruitful area. Memphis was a lot better. Still, I was missing a lot of key pieces.

And then I did a radio program and the New Orleans material began to come out on record and I did that five volume series called *The Music of New Orleans* that came out on Folkways in the late 50's--it came out about '59, I guess--it started with the Eureka Brass Band. So, I was asked to do a radio program in New York about the Eureka Brass Band and New Orleans jazz. My first book had come out, Jazz New Orleans, and there was a lot of attention given to it--a lot of abuse--because I had opened up a lot of people to this world. So, I was asked to do a radio program with Gunther Schuller and Nat Hentoff on WBAI, and at the end of the program we talked about New Orleans, about jazz, and Nat Hentoff said to me "So, what are you doing now?" and I said "I'm really working on the blues. I'm so excited, there's this wonderful thing that nobody knows anything about," and he says "Are you looking for a publisher?" And I said "Yes." And he said, well, here's a name--Ted Aspesson at Rinehart--he's looking for something like that, so why don't you bring it by?" That was a Sunday night. By Thursday, I think, I'd written five chapters and I handed the five chapters to Ted Aspesson--they were a bit sketchy! They were on Blind Willie Johnson (I'd picked the people I'd already been doing research on) and wrote up my notes--the Memphis Jug Band...So, that was Thursday, and I was living in a sculptor's pad on Broadway in the Village, just scraping by since I had no money and worked as a picture framer. On Monday there was a telegram in my downstairs mailbox saying "We accept the book and have an English publisher, when can you come sign the contract?" So, I thought--my life's work--I thought "Wow, this is easy!"

So then I got, I think, a $250 advance! Phew, I mean, we're talking really heavy money! So, Ann and I were together and she was busy recording the Scott Joplin for me--the first serious Joplin recordings. We were busy doing that and so I borrowed her little Chevrolet coupe and took the advance and headed South to simply do research on the blues and did this long, long, long research trip that took me all the way through the South, back through New Orleans, all through Texas looking for Blind Lemon, all the way up through St. Louis, to Chicago, and back to New York. And it is out of those notes, and material I'd previously gathered, plus my knowledge of recordings, which--beginning in the mid to late 40s I really knew the recordings pretty cold. And then--I'm embarrassed to say it--but I wrote the book in 36 days. I was so filled with the subject and I just wrote it--it just came out white hot! When people have asked me to revise it--no one asked me to revise it [at the time], they always said they liked it--well, I should, because it was full of mistakes. But, I can't match the passion. It's full of mistakes, but I absolutely cannot match what I put into it. It just came sweeping out. We were living in this little basement apartment in Brooklyn and working on the ragtime--Joe Lamb, the last of the great ragtime composers would come into the house--wonderful Joe--and he'd play rags for us. I was playing banjo with Dave van Ronk in various jug bands (we made a record in '58). In '58 Annie and I had been down in the Bahamas...We were just recording a ton of music! We were recording Charles Ives for Folkways.

MI: Why for Folkways?

CHARTERS: Well, because they were available. And Moe--Moe was the only person I knew whose vision was even bigger than mine. Moe's vision was so large that it encompassed all our visions: Fred Ramsey's, mine. We all fit into this large, large, view that Moe had of what the world had created and how he would document it. So, Moe was available and he would put things out quickly and he'd keep them in the catalogue. So, I could work for other companies, and I did, but it was always a can of worms. You had meetings, you had to sit down and talk about things, they'd want to participate--Moe, I simply gave him the edited tapes and the notes and three months later there was the record. And I liked the covers! Ron Kline did a super job. He became the designer so Ronnie and I were very close friends. So, Ronnie would take old photos I'd found and just turn them into masterpieces. And we really--it was something that we all believed in. Fred Ramsey lived in New Jersey--I was seeing Fred all the time and he was as obsessed with early jazz as I was. He had this unbelievable collection of old 78s that he'd compiled in 1925 when he was at Princeton. And my model, as a writer, was Charles Edward Smith, the first major jazz writer, who had written in *Jazzmen*.

MI: I was just looking in *Jazzmen* this morning and it strikes me--I can see it now that you say it, but it never occurred to me before I looked at them. How did you get to know these guys? When?

CHARTERS: Well...of course, being an intellectual fellow, when I realized in California that people weren't understanding jazz I thought I'd better tell 'em about jazz! So I went and got every jazz book out of the library--there weren't so many (I think there were three)--but *Jazzmen*...You can't believe the effect that *Jazzmen* had on us! I think for a lot of younger people *The Country Blues* had the same effect. *Jazzmen* just stunned us--as you know, I named the continuation of *The Country Blues*, I called it *Bluesmen* as a tribute to Fred. And then the people who'd done this and who'd recorded Bunk Johnson--that was a whole crowd, Bill Russell, Fred Ramsey, everybody--these were just legends to me. These were the men who had--it was like a map of the New World! I mean, here was somebody who provided me with a first sort've clumsy map into a world that I felt was so real and so incredibly exciting. They were the first map, the first chart, that told us how to get in. So, *Jazzmen* was enormously influential. Had it not come immediately before the war its effect would have been immediately felt. But it came just before and everybody put things aside.

Then in 1954, when I was living in New Orleans, I finally started my research as a picture framer doing odd jobs and things. I was always around the French Quarter, various scams involving tourists and picture frames--you know, those charcoal portrait sketches: you know, great high art! So, Fred Ramsey came through and we were all--all of us who were in the New Orleans jazz world , we all knew each other. People would come through--any artist or painter or freelancer or photographer--they'd all come through, they'd check first with Dick Allen, then Dick Allen would let me know and so we'd know everybody. Fred Ramsey came to town with a wife and a new child and needed a place to stay so we immediately had to help Fred to find a place. So, how to deal with, for me, with one of the legends, Frederick Ramsey, Jr., who had done the Leadbelly last sessions, he had done the 12 volume re-issue series on Folkways of jazz--Fred was the role model! And there he was! It was hot, and it was sweaty, and we just lay around drinking beer and his wife and kid took sick and had to go back, so Fred was alone. And Fred was playing me all of these tapes, he was playing me the first tapes of those crazy brass bands from Alabama, and we talked and we talked and we talked.

And from Fred, I must say, that after I talked to him my respect for what they had done had gone up. Because they fought the real battles in the 30's and 40's when it was real bad. They had all been dragged through every kind of political investigation--they all had been, like me, seriously involved in the whole culture, not just blues and jazz. Fred had been to Paris, his Master's thesis at Princeton was on Joyce, and he met Joyce! So, he was deeply into French culture, he was bilingual. He also trained as a composer, a serious composer, and he had a fair degree of success with his early percussion works in the 1920s and he set out to write a concerto for trumpet and percussion and someone played him a Louis Armstrong record and he never looked back! It was not only that we were all obsessed with jazz, but we were all obsessed with larger cultural questions. We were endlessly involved with everything.

MI: What kind of investigations are you talking about? I haven't heard any of this. Fred Ramsey and the others--were they being investigated as leftists or something?

CHARTERS: We were all involved in anti-American activities--being associated with Folkways was a Red channel. So, we were investigated. Leadbelly, as you know, was investigated, and Fred had recorded Leadbelly. Russell had--Russell was an incredibly complicated man. He had put out those AM records--I don't know if you've ever seen any of the originals--they're these little 10 inch records and he did put notes saying these were made on poor recording equipment but that was the best that was available during the existing military dictatorship. And there was another set of notes that said: These were recorded during one of America's frequent wars for freedom abroad. We were all really out front, and in those days the South was still legally segregated and when I would hang out with musicians I had to tell everybody I was a full-blooded Indian--I didn't really look Cherokee but I was. Otherwise, everybody in the place was obliged to have me arrested.

So, then we all come through this, we're all politically pretty united, and we were all passionately committed and in love with jazz. So, with Fred I had to learn first the techniques. He had actually taken his love and translated it into a book and then on to Folkways Records. He lived in New Jersey and Ann and I went to see him a lot. We stopped to see him on the way down to the Bahamas. So Fred was very important and the writer Charles Smith--when Charlie would come down to meet Fred ...His pieces on Pee Wee Russell were just models of how to do it. We would go to a bar and Charlie would order two drinks and we would order one...One of the guys, Gene Williams, who was very closely associated with Bill and Fred in bringing Bunk to new York--Bunk endlessly complained about what they'd done to him, you know, gotten him out of the country there and brought him to New York to play for all these white people with a bunch of musicians who are really terrible! He hated that band! He thought they were the biggest bunch of lunks, couldn't play anything! He said these incredibly racist, ugly things about that wonderful, marvelous band that turned the world around! But Bunk hated them! So one of the guys, Eugene Williams, one of the guys in the group, took it so seriously that he killed himself. We're talking passion!

And at the same time, on the other side of us, is the Bop revolution. Here, something had happened that we all had to deal with in very complicated ways. At the same time in the 1950s I'm in New Orleans doing research and New York is going crazy. It was not we who had to deal with it, but all the New Orleans musicians had to deal with it. We could never really sit still and just be content to do a little work in New Orleans--it was swirling around us, these incredible changes in African-American music. And when we would go to the clubs you're hearing all of the R & B--we were listening to Ruth Brown. We were listening to Little Milton and Ruth Brown, and these groups would come through town and play in these clubs in the middle of the black neighborhoods and by God we managed to get in. In a way it sounds like we were just a bunch of fuddy-duddies but that was not it--it was much more complex than that. And as I say, through the work of these early pioneers we learned not only what was there to be done but they also showed us tools and how to work them.

MI: Well, what did you think about Bop?

CHARTERS: It's very simple to explain. Guys like me, we were really quite green. I didn't do dope; I had a family problem so I didn't even drink until I was in my mid-twenties after I got out of the Army, actually! And we, of course, found out about musicians. We listened to Jazz at the Philharmonic, and they really scared us. Their way of life--it's easy now to look back but if you're dealing with a 26 year-old heroin addict looking at you across the microphone and he can't even focus his eyes you're having real troubles with this. They were in and out of prison, the music was incredibly controversial, and yet it was fascinating. I was so aware that it was "blacker" than the New Orleans music--that history got turned upside down--that the things that the Boppers were doing were closer to African-American roots than the very refined, white and black mix, of the music of New Orleans.

So, for myself, I recognized by the mid-50s that the New Orleans musicians were dealing as best they could--generally saying you can't hear the melody. A trombone player came down from Eastman to play--there was a group of modernists living with us in the French Quarter, hanging out at 912, the famous 912 that Kerouac hung out in, Bill Burroughs was living across the river--and hanging out in the French Quarter with us was a group of modernists. Johnny Elgin played piano, Mouse played the sax, Bruce Lippincott played the sax, and so we were aware that there was Bop because they kept playing it! They were rehearsing in the courtyard and they listened to it. So, I think it was about '55 or '56 that a trombone player from Eastman came down named Paul Crawford and Paul and I worked out a deal with young ladies where we would paint their apartments in exchange for free beer and a chance to listen to their records. So, Paul and I spent many, many days together and I finally said "Paul, I gotta know about this new music. It was like I had to know about Rap. So Paul very carefully took me through Bop so that by '57 I was current.

And also I was hearing Elvis out of the juke boxed in the black neighborhoods thinking "This is pretty incredible!" And also when I came to New York in '58 you heard it everywhere in New York, every Bop musician, every one of them, playing at their peak. There was

Mingus, there was Miles--you know, all going on--and of course, all the people like Mulligan--it was a mixture of white and black, and you never knew what they were going to do next. It was really cheap, you'd go and sit all night and it was wonderful. I rounded a corner in a little club, the Half Note, and there was Annie pinned against the wall by Charlie--Mingus had just stabbed his wife, you know?--and I thought "What the hell is this all about?" and I get over there and the two of them are having this incredibly excited conversation about Jelly Roll Morton! It was a wild, crazy time. This was one of the drawbacks--there was very, very little blues in New York. There was Brownie and Sonny and there was the Rev. [Gary Davis], and the Rev. was busy turning on all of those guitar players--he really founded the whole New York revivalist guitar school. Between Brownie and the Rev. it's all there--all the finger-picking.

MI: So, when you were there you didn't see much interaction between jazz and blues and stuff like that?

CHARTERS: Well, the jazz musicians were so into their own excitement! I mean, if you're inventing Bop, you don't have a lot of time to listen to 12 bar blues! And as far as they were concerned, they had grown up with the traditional orchestral blues, so blues for them was Jimmy Rushing and it was the Count Basie Orchestra. It certainly was not Ellington ...They hardly played blues at all, and they played them badly. The Basie band--Jesus Christ, it was one blues after another! They blew their asses off! So, for the orchestral musicians, sure, blues is okay, but as far as they were concerned--the African-American young Bopper--the blues was an old-timey pop music. They'd grown up hearing the stuff, you know, and it was just love songs off in the background and it didn't really mean a hell of a lot.

MI: What did you think about someone like Miles--you know, Cool and that stuff?

CHARTERS: Well, you know, Miles was an interesting case. From the beginning he was incredibly distinctive and one of the things about Miles was in a world of incredibly brilliant technicians Miles couldn't play very well. Miles was okay, but he couldn't really do it all and he was reluctant to follow Charlie sometimes, you know, because Parker would call changes in the middle of a set--I never saw him with Parker, I saw him with Cannon Ball and Coltrane--but they say that in the middle of a number Parker would want rhythm changes and Miles would either not be able to do it or not want to do it. In fact, Parker replaced Miles with Red Rodney, the white guy, who could do it. And when you listen to the 50s there is this incredible decimation of great trumpet players: Clifford was killed, Fats Navarro died very young, Booker Little died very young. So, we have a very unbalanced view of what the 50s were like--had they lived we wouldn't have this sense that the only thing going on was Miles.

There's a wonderful recording--I don't know if you've heard it--where Miles is there with an orchestra with Monk and everybody and they're doing "The Man I Love," and Miles begins with this incredibly soupy half rhythm [hums and laughs]--and what comes next? Monk goes on the piano [hums same soupy rhythm satirically] and then he runs and hides in the toilet! And you can hear all of this shouting in the background--they put everything out in those days, you know, if they recorded it they had to put it out--and Monk refused to come out and he thought the whole thing was just ridiculous. After all the fighting and struggling they'd done to go back to [hums soupy rhythm]! But even then Miles was very tough--back to the audience using the mute. The whole band was so full of heroin they couldn't even find each other on the bandstand. You have no idea the amount of drugs! Well, if you went through the 60s rock thing you've seen the same amount of drugs.

MI: I was born in '63.

CHARTERS: Oh, then you didn't see it. But whew! I was out in San Francisco doing Country Joe and the amount of drugs was unbelievable! Just unbelievable. It's always been a part of this Dionysian streak. One thing we always loved about the musicians is that some of them would go to the edge and those are the ones we remember. Those who didn't, we don't. That's why we love Robert Johnson--he went as close to the edge as you can. Then died, thank heavens, before he could make 10,000 recordings all sounding like himself.

MI: That's right--like Hooker.

CHARTERS: Or Big Bill. Even the last session that Robert did--with "Malted Milk Blues" and things, it was getting very thin. The great ones come in the first.

MI: Through all this, of course--I was just looking through your wife's Portable Kerouac (or whatever) the other day--and I assume that you guys were involved with a lot of these [Beat] folks and they, of course, were all interested in jazz. Did that also play a part in this or was it more like you were teaching them or something?

CHARTERS: Well, we did have a period in the 60s--but by this time things had settled down--Allen Ginsberg would come over a lot and wanted us to play blues for him--so we sort've helped with Allen's education with blues. But at that point we were all out in the Beat area, the whole Beat crowd. Annie was living in a cottage half a mile from where Allen was living in a cottage and Gary Snyder's cottage was about five blocks away. Annie, as you probably read in that book, dated Peter Orlovsky and went down and heard the first full reading of "Howl" in Berkeley. I was there with another girl and Annie was there with Peter Orlovsky! I had published my first book of poetry in '53 and then when I was living in San Francisco saving money to go to New Orleans my neighbors across the street were going to start a bookstore and I was doing credit checking for Dun and Bradstreet so I was given special permission to start a credit report on their efforts to start a bookstore even though it wasn't in my area--and that was City Lights Bookstore. I wrote the credit report that got them all their books! They had no money at all, Peter and everybody, we were all sort've scuffling along the same way.

You're probably getting a sense of what kind of community we were. We were all linked and as I've said it wasn't only the blues. We were listening to Indian classical music, we were listening to Finnish music--we were really into alternatives. The 50s was hard to deal with. And we really had to find some way that was different. We explored everything--Charles Ives' music. We would have weekends in New York when we would simply open up the house...and anybody who wanted to play would simply write on the blackboard what piece they were going to play and we'd listen to it. It was a tiny community, we all knew each other, and we all shuffled between Greenwich Village, the French Quarter, and North Beach, and there was so much going on. Action painting was going on and the involvement with jazz was so intense--people don't realize that in San Francisco in the 40s the painters were all abstract expressionists--they called it First

Sensation--a wonderful term, isn't it?--and then the first figurative painting was a David Park painting--they're all playing in a jazz band. It's a portrait from the piano of all the San Francisco artists playing in a jazz band! Albert Bischoff's playing trumpet! So, all of us who were playing jazz then--I was playing four or five nights a week to make money--and everyone was a part of it: the painters were a part of this, the poets were a part of this, everything was being published underground, we had no publishers. We were all circulating. We were all part of this thing that was going on, we had no idea what the results would be, but we were pursuing every aspect of it. The Boppers? Certainly, we recognized them but it's hard to include New Orleans jazz and Bop.

MI: Did you have a sense of Bop in the late 40s?

CHARTERS: Oh absolutely. As I say, having been involved with jazz all my life, in the late 40s I was a 20 year-old professional jazz musician. I knew everything that was going on. One thing I really have to say is that Bop was really hard to play. It was really hard stuff. Whatever I thought about it there was no way I could ever play it. This was hard to give up because I really thought, if I found the right instrument--clarinet wasn't right and I'd switched to rhythm instruments--I could have a meaningful jazz career. When I heard the Boppers that was it! There was no way that I could perform what they were performing. They were just so good. They were scary...We were aware of it, we were aware of every tremor because there wasn't a hell of a lot going on.

MI: What does that mean? There's not a hell of a lot going on? You mean like the rest of the culture is producing --

CHARTERS: Absolutely! Jimmy Simms, Jo Stafford--it was pretty white bread! It wasn't our reality. This happens in popular music often. What they had done describes perfectly the democratization of the society in the 20s [operatic style to a more chatty one]...A lot of things had happened and I was born in 1929 and I grew up with this music. And I felt it defined--and for a time it did, for the first twenty years of my life it did adequately define reality: the sexual relationships, the ambitions. Pop music we use as a way to define ourselves and as a way to exchange sexual information, what is expected in a relationship--it's too crude to say 'sexual information'--

how to define the relationships we wish to have with the opposite sex. It's the most instantly communicable set of material we have. Pop music instantly conveys should you be jealous? should you not be jealous? You know, the questions are endlessly resolved in pop music, and that's where we get our answers more than anywhere else. And that's one reason why for the young people it's so crucial. For the first twenty years Bing Crosby did define that and then suddenly in the 50s the world changed and the pop music didn't define it any more.

And we initially made a mistake: because initially we thought folk music would do it. The blues, we recognized, was not ours, and so we didn't dream of performing it. We could see it, we were conscious of it, but it was like Bach--it was too distant; it came with too many different cultural attributes even though we passionately loved it. In those days all we could do with guitars was strum the damn things! I remember I came to New York in 1958 and I would sit there with van Ronk who played guitar then and we sat together and tried to finger pick. And Dave could do it a little better than the rest of us--but not much! We were all into strums and union songs because we were intensely political. The 50s was fought on the battle of politics, and so suddenly, when Bobby Dylan politicized it for us then it all fell in place. And then in the mid-60s it became possible to create a new pop music which would define the new social situation. That's why it took over and that's why it continues to define what we do today.

MI: You know, when you think about the sort of society you were looking at and trying to think of alternatives to it in the US in the 50s, what was writing a book about blues going to help you do?

CHARTERS: Well, for me it is on two levels. First was a desire to play a role in public affairs--and I studied at the University of International Relations for three years. The other level is that I ran afoul of the McCarthy committee and I was declared disloyal in 1952 when I was in the Army and transferred from my job at an Army newspaper to a front line ski unit where I spent some time in various holes at 58 degrees below zero waiting for Russians to attack. So, what I had hoped would be a public role, I hoped with the United Nations--I studied, as I say, three years at the University of International Relations--and when this happened suddenly I could never even run for public office; I could never hold any government job. So I had been effectively removed from any sort of public role.

For me, the writing about black music was my way of fighting racism. That's why my work is not academic, that is why it is absolutely nothing but popularization: I wanted people to hear black music, as I said in *The Poetry of the Blues*, which was a tremendous best-seller, and is the most open and the most blatantly political of my books, and that's why I've never permitted it to be republished.

MI: Because you think the context is no longer appropriate?

CHARTERS: That's right. I mean, God, the Blackstone Rangers carried copies around in their back pockets ...It literally sold hundreds of thousands. It's where I say, you know, if by introducing music I can have somebody look across the racial divide and see a black face and see this person as a human being--and that's why my work is unashamedly romantic. It absolutely destroyed any credibility I would ever have in the academy. I was often asked to lecture in the 60s and I did give a series of lectures at Yale, seminars and things. I was offered many academic posts. When I did see that I was going to give my life to this, I did take some courses at the University of California in music theory and music history--I was not a bumpkin who didn't know musically what I was talking about, and I always thought this was crucial. It may seem a round-about way to effect a revolution but it was the only way I could do it. I'm not Allen Ginsberg! As Allen and I have found out many times. But the one time I really did set out--there were many of us--I set out to burn the White House! I did have burning materials in my pocket, I fought through police lines, and I was on national television with this ring of busses surrounding the White House and I was the only one who got far enough to see that on the lawn of the White House there were 3,000 troops with draw bayonets.

MI: When was this?

CHARTERS: This was right after the Kent State killings. But while we were doing this Allen was chanting for us and the only sounds we could hear above the shouts of the police and the tear gas was the sound of Allen's voice. So, Allen did it his way, I did it mine. We were doing the same thing.

MI: So, in the aftermath of the problems with HUAC you were disabled. How did they justify this attack on you?

CHARTERS: I had been in Paris in 1948, as a teenager, and Communists attempted to take over the government--there was armed fighting on the streets of Paris while I was there. So, I wrote dumb little amateur articles about this which appeared in the *Sacramento Bee*. And because I got so interested in it I went to the big rallies that Maurice Thorez was having before everybody hit the streets. I was actively anti-Communist because I was so disturbed by the Communist take-over in Czechoslovakia. I was really anti-Communist, but I was there at these rallies and I did write these little, dumb letters, these articles, that the *Sacramento Bee* published saying I'd been there. And so you were asked when you came in the Army, asking whether you had ever been a member of, of had you ever attended a meeting, of the Communist Party. So I went to the officer and said something and he just said "Just say yes and sign it." So I did! And then I was investigated and it saved my life. The company I trained with was pulled back--we did basic training 14 weeks then we had a 30 day leave--and they pulled them back after ten days and flew them directly to Korea and threw them into a battle against the Chinese and with one exception they were all killed. I met the one sole survivor who'd been on buddy assignment with me--I met him later.

They kept me as a semi-prisoner--having no idea what was going on--breaking rocks on the Presidio Military Compound in Monterey. And I was alone in the company area when the Sergeant called and said :"Hey Charters! All those guys? You know, they're all dead." I thought wow, had it not been for this political entanglement I'd be just as dead as they were. And I didn't find out about it until, as I say, a guy who was in college with me who was on assignment said "Hey, you're in trouble, I'm going to get you out of here. You want to go to Alaska?" I said 'Well, okay..."

So I was shipped with the Youth Representative of the American Socialist Party--the two of us were put in with a black engineering company and shipped to Alaska. And I met my high school track coach there who said, "I'm going to put you on the post newspaper." Then I had to get a security clearance--the newspaper came out once a week and I wrote about sports! For this, you had to get a security clearance...Then it all came out and they marched me into a room full of Lt.-Colonels, sat me down, and said, "Son, you've been accused of disloyalty --private charges of disloyalty but you have to answer them." I sort've looked incredulous, said, "What am I accused of?" and they said "That's secret material, we can't reveal that." [laughs] So then they then placed in my files--after much fruitless talking--they placed a letter in my files that said I'd been disloyal. Then I figured that once they'd done this to me--then I got involved with Folkways and everything and said "Well, okay, I'll be disloyal!" [laughs] The first time I protested the Vietnam War I went down to Washington--it was '65--and there were 30 of us. There were so few of us that this one leader told us all to kneel on the sidewalks and we all kneeled on the sidewalks and the FBI came and took close-up photos of us. Then the next time I went down, it was after Kent State, and there were 100,000 of us and I was going to burn the fucking White House down--and then two months later I left the country. I just realized that the War was beginning to be too just--I was either going to join the Weathermen...And I was 40 years old, I had a wife and child, and the Weathermen were not for me. So, I left the country instead. Without a regret in the world.

MI: I can imagine. I've often wanted to myself.

CHARTERS: Oh yes!

MI: So, you were not even a Communist Party member and they were treating you like one.

CHARTERS: I was actually, throughout this whole active period, rather reluctantly anti-Communist. In the 50s you didn't dare be political. And also, while I was in basic training we were given an hour of political indoctrination every day. They often spoke about freedom and inevitably I would stand up and say, "I've been to the South, I've seen legal segregation," I'd say "how can you talk about freedom when in the South Negroes are being treated like..." And I'd look over and see people writing this down. So, simply to challenge segregation laws...

I mean, people don't understand! I spent a year in Europe after the *Country Blues* came out--came back in '61-- and Ken Goldstein sent me South to Memphis to record Furry. And I thought "Well, I've been all over Europe, maybe I'll see America"--feeling all sentimental.

So, I took a train. The train went through Washington--you won't believe this--but we got off outside of Washington and the train stopped in a field, and every Negro passenger got up and went to a car in the back!. You won't believe it! This is legal! I looked at this, and I'd just spent a year in Europe, and just trying to deal with all these things, and so I went back--and tacked on the back of this sleek, streamlined, new train were these filthy, dirty old railroad coaches, they're barely lit, there's no running water, and there was every African-American passenger. They had to get out and walk along the side of the tracks to get back to this car!

MI: Because they were entering segregated territory.

CHARTERS: Yes. Right. 1961! Right outside of Washington, DC. I mean, there was this endless crap about segregation! It was there. Annie and I were pursued by the police, we were stopped, our cameras were taken, we lived through the days of the registration drives--we were terrified! People have no idea. It's over now--the worst of it's over, and the South is a different place. But Jesus, I mean, I did research on Robert Johnson in Robertsonville, Mississippi, I thought I'd just go back to the old way of just talking to people on the street. So, I would talk to somebody, looked the right age, might know somebody like Robert Johnson, and they would talk and then following me were the sheriff and a deputy and anyone I talked to they were pinning them up against a tree! I said "Who needs--I'm not going to do this to people." I'm sure you read the thing when we were recording Baby Tate in Spartanburg and suddenly we looked out the window and there was the sheriff with a drawn pistol and a deputy with a drawn pistol--one coming in the front one coming in the back. And they banged in the door and stood there with their drawn pistols looking at us and there was Annie with her notebook, I was holding a microphone next to a tape recorder, and there was Baby Tate with a guitar. And the sheriff looks at us and says: "I hear you're selling bootleg liquor in here." And they searched the house. You know--up and down, it was a little two-story frame house, they searched the whole thing, not saying a word, and we're still sitting there, unmoving, because these guys had guns. People disappeared in the South a lot. And then he came downstairs and looked at me and looked at Baby

Tate, took the guitar, and then as he went out the door he said, "They sure got rhythm, don't they?"

Fred Ramsey went down to do a documentary for CBS--"Hear Me Talkin' to Ya"--and they had set up microphones around a black baptism or something like this, and over the microphones suddenly they picked up Klan members planning to rush Fred and kill him! They just carefully shut down the microphones, announced he was going to move on, and decided this wasn't such a good idea after all and got the hell out of there. It's all so gentle, now, but you can't believe the way it was only a generation ago.

MI: What happened when you went to talk--when you went to Memphis? When you went to talk to Will Shade, Furry, Gus Cannon, all of those guys?

CHARTERS: Well, it was always very clear-cut with me: I was always their record man. And that was a known relationship, was very specific, it had beginnings and endings, and if anything else happened--if I wanted to get drunk with them that was okay. Most of the time they called me "Mr." Mr. Sam. I hear tapes when they're talking to me, and they say "Mr. Sam..." Gus Cannon, to be sure, called all of us "White Folk." "White Folk, I'd like to know..." He was going to make absolutely sure that he never stepped over the lines. But after recording them, I would go up into the ghettos in Detroit and Cleveland and Chicago and I'd go into a club where I wasn't known to hear a band like Mighty Joe Young--we were going to hear him in one of the really bad areas in the south of Chicago--I'd take records with me. I'd take LPs and I'd put them on the table, and usually whatever gang was running that club--or was in charge of that club--and then finally one of the young guys would get up and walk over to the table and look at me, he'd look at the records, and he'd look at the records and turn them over and he'd say, "So, you make records?" I'd say yes, then he'd go back. That was an accepted way to enter the black community. Otherwise you were involved with drugs or you were an underground police informer or you're after black women and there's no other reason to be there. Those neighborhoods are no fun and nobody's going to believe you're there for the view or the food. If you had a specific reason--I was recording on the South Side at Johnny Pepper's the gangs would begin to gather, they would give us a certain amount of leeway to get the equipment up, then after a certain hour the streets were theirs. We had accepted this, understood it, and when the moment came, get! Johnny could protect us to a certain extent but after that he couldn't protect us and we had to get out.

MI: You know, the attempt to get people to look at black people as just a person--I assume that's what you mean when you say to look across color lines?

CHARTERS: That's right.

MI: Is that why you decided--I was just reading something that was being abusive about treating blues as poetry--is that why you chose to treat it as poetry?

CHARTERS: Absolutely. Absolutely. There was, in the white tradition, the tradition of the *poete maudit*, the wild, rebel poet...And really, growing up in my time, of course, we had Henry Miller, you know, sneaking in these sex books! So, you know, the blues--I'm a poet myself. I'm essentially a poet, and everything else fits around the emotional center that is that I write a lot of poetry. So I thought in terms of this sort--I thought in terms of poetry. And to find in the blues a very small, but very pure, strain of folk poetry which was really very exciting. Then to find it diluted and watered down and abused and finally just turned into another commercial, surgically shaped, product was why I stopped being interested. But the initial purity of Charley Patton lyrics and Blind Willie McTell lyrics--these magnificent, long, extended metaphors in Lonnie Johnson's lyrics. It's wonderful! Most people still weren't hearing it. I must say that I got so bored--I really got incredibly bored with all those damn guitar solos. To me they all sounded like B.B. King and what I really wanted to hear was great text, and I have not, lately, been hearing enough great text. [laughs]

MI: So, what did you think about R & B in the 50s and 60s and all that?

CHARTERS: R & B was a hell of a lot of fun. Along with going downtown to the clubs to hear the jazz we were all going to hear--not all of us--Danny Kalb and I were going up to the Apollo Theater to hear the R & B, and geez, you know, things like "High Heel Sneakers" came along, and WOW! There we were! So, we heard all the R & B we could. I'll never forget Louis Jordan and Tympani Five surrounded by strobe lights looking as if they were suspended in space with them brown and white shoes! We were into the whole package. I was attempting to find record companies to record James P. Johnson's piano concerto, the whole thing. That's why we were putting out Scott Joplin--we did everything but coon songs, which we could have done but we didn't.

And so, of course, we were hearing a lot of R & B but it didn't need us. I always had the feeling that there were so few of us and the work so vast. That's why I wrote the books as I did--to romanticize the glamour of looking for old blues singers. I was saying "Help! This job is really big and I really need lots of help!" I really exaggerated this but it worked! My God, I came back from that year in Europe and I found kids doing research in the South. It was the most magnificent research project, really, I could think of. Without pay, usually without real knowledge of how to do it, they found everything...If we hadn't done that work--all those wonderful kids like George Mitchell, who came to see me in the mid-60s. They almost all came to me at some point, they wrote me a letter saying this is what I'm doing. Some of them hated me and some of them said they were going to sue me...but they all checked in with me! At some point or another everyone came to me to get the seal of approval, like Chris Strachwitz and everything, and off they went. And it was wonderful! I had no jealousy. It was too big!

I was only going to make four records! My dream was to make four records: I was going to do Blind Willie Johnson, I was going to do the Eureka Brass Band, I was going to do the Six and Seven Eighths String Orchestra of New Orleans, and I was going to do the Scott Joplin Bouquet, and that was it! Annie and I were living in a flop house on the lower East side with thousands of cockroaches and three of the albums were out--everything but the Joplin...And I was going to quit doing albums, and say this thirty years later! [laughs] It just worked out that way. There was too much exciting music, too many stories to find out, too much to follow. I couldn't really step away...

My feeling was that whatever these people may have thought about our methods or our reasons for doing the research, these people were dying and there were no written records. If we didn't do it; if we didn't interview the survivors and they died, there would be no story. I did a big book in Sweden, the first book that had ever been done on

Swedish folk fiddlers, people who occupied the same role as blues singers: these were the drunks, the down-and outs, the crazies who passed on a magnificent body of folk music. And what I found in Sweden, unlike in the United States, was that this had done by members of the society. Even though they were down-and-out they were members of the society, so there was documentation. Every little village had some little memory, record, archive--I would find written materials from 1740, I'd find photo archives, newspapers. It's just unbelievable what I found. But here's America where these were blacks, nothing was to be found. It was miserable. If we didn't get interviews, if we didn't talk to people, there'd be nothing. There'd be no way ever to recreate the story. So I figured, "What the hell! Whatever your motivations are out there doing interviews with old bluesmen, just get the interviews right. Figure out your reasons later but get the names and the dates and see what they've done."

MI: Try to give me an idea what went on when you first met some guy like--I'm just thinking of the three guys in Memphis like Will Shade, Furry Lewis, and Gus Cannon. What was it like when you walk into this? Was Will Shade living in that apartment on Fourth and Beale or whatever?

CHARTERS: Yeah, they were very poor. He did, occasionally, see white people because he would play little parties with the jug band, so he knew what happened and he had sort've an informal way to approach everybody. So with Will, there was never quite the point where he'd dropped out. He'd had a long recording career--twelve years when he'd been recording. So, to Will it was a very familiar situation.

With someone like Furry Lewis, who hadn't seen anybody in 30 years, this was enormous! It was like: "Wow, you're interested in that old stuff? Well...You're really interested in that old stuff? You really are interested in that old stuff?" Then he'd call--he'd say "Hey, there's a man here--there's this white boy who's really interested in that old stuff! You know that stuff I used to do? There's this white boy who's really interested." So it was impossible for me to have any really close, private meeting with these guys. For one thing, they didn't want to be one-to-one with a white person, but the other thing is they wanted ever body else to know! It was as if they hadn't been lying all these years! Because their own society was totally into rhythm and blues or the Mills Brothers. I mean, people from our point of view don't realize, as I've said before, how marginal the blues was even in the black community. It was really, really, marginal.

MI: Now, that's not popular to say these days.

CHARTERS: No, but I was there. I was listening to the juke box, and I never heard a real blues record on a juke box. They just didn't know it--they knew R & B. Because along with everything else, blues projected an image that was really pretty down! I mean, these were helpless, beat up people. Whereas in the 40s with the work in the war plants, the great record of the black GIs in the War, there was a pride in the community. I t wasn't yet shaped and focused the way it has become, but there was a pride. They'd stood up and they'd been counted, they'd heard, and they'd done something. And also they were proud of jazz, they knew about Duke Ellington--they knew about all this. They had their R & B and R & B was wonderful. They loved being in the zoot suits, the bands were great to watch. I used to go down to a little club in Sacramento that had white jazz one week and black R & B the next. I'd hear groups like the Jive Bombers! They were wonderful! I mean, Cement Mixer Putty-Putty was marvelous. So, in the black community they shared our same feeling that someone like Furry Lewis was really from another time.

MI: Did they believe that he was really a musician?

CHARTERS: Of course not! Nor could they believe that at any time anyone had really taken this seriously. There was absolutely no historical sense. Within poor industrial communities people are scattered from roots. There is no sense of tradition. It isn't there. You're simply being entertained. In the rural areas where there's continuing tradition, poverty doesn't mean there's no tradition. Absolutely not. The villages I visited in Africa were governed by centuries of tradition. But in industrial ghettos, in any color in any society, in any city in the world, there is no focus for tradition.

So, for someone like Furry, even if they sort've believed him, it didn't really make any difference at all. No one would take him seriously. And the fact that a white person was coming! It became incredibly poignant when Anne was with me because many of these musicians, like Memphis Willie B., were married and were living really solid, middle class lives. And I shall never forget--Ann came with me and we went and had a social evening in Memphis Willie B.'s house with his wife. And this was the first time in her life that Memphis Willie B.'s wife had sat socially and talked equally with a white woman. And at the end of the evening she broke down sobbing because of what it had meant to her. We were trying so desperately not to seem patronizing or anything and just be one on one--to present ourselves that way. And I wasn't--the way many of the younger kids did--came on too strong. I always kept the role that I'm here for a limited amount of time, I'm here for a short visit, how wonderful to see you; and I'd signed Willie B. to a contract with Prestige and we'd hoped he'd have a career, so the role was clear and defined. Or I'd go to Henry Townsend when he was living in one of the projects in St. Louis--and again, it was this thing where a white person was just coming and sitting at the kitchen table. They thought this was just incredible! When I worked in St. Louis in the early 1960s I worked, actually, with a cop who loved the blues--Lt. Charlie O'Brien.

MI: Oh yeah--Koester told me about him.

CHARTERS: That's right. And he knew where everybody was. And a couple of times--I guess this was over in East St. Louis where Miles was from--it was a little tricky and Charlie would just let everybody notice the revolver in his waist band. When we would go to see a blues singer he just couldn't break a habit--there would be the three swift knocks and then the jump to the side of the door, then "Hey, we want to come in!" And I'd be saying "Oh shit!", but it always worked; the doors always opened! You never knew what was on the other side of the door. You can kind've get the idea why we often had the feeling that the blues came out of a completely other world.

MI: That's what Koester was saying to me, too.

CHARTERS: Yeah, the feeling that it was another world, and to get that deeply into the black community was--you were really a stranger! You were really a stranger. Not at risk, because in those days they would rob you, but they didn't dare hurt you, because they figured that the police would come crashing down. It was later in the 60s that it got to be really dangerous, really dangerous, phew! Now it's more dangerous than it ever was. You just don't go there. The black singers are leaving the ghetto, also...When I first met Rockin' Dukesy and I started working with him he was living down in an area of trailers and things in a poor neighborhood, and then after we started making records and he started to make more money he bought for cash (I have no idea what his tax situation was) but he paid in crumpled dollar bills, for a $95,000 house in the nicest white neighborhood in Lafayette, Louisiana. So, the rest of the time I saw Dukesy I went there! Living in those ghetto areas is no good for anybody.

MI: I know that Roger Brown, you know, George's buddy, was telling me that when they--I guess it was in '61?--they bought that Memphis Willie B. you put out and they read the liner notes, and they read notes in there where you said something about talking to Will Shade; and that Will Shade put you onto Memphis Willie B.; and they said well, if he can go find Will Shade and talk to him, then, by God, we can go talk to him! And they, within a few months, got into the car and drove over to Memphis.

CHARTERS: It was the same thing for Charlie Musselwhite. He said well, it's gotta be easy! Once I showed people that you could go there--it was wonderful! They went! What a thing to do--you can strike a blow for freedom and equality for mankind by listening to blues and passing a joint! It was perfect! It was the easiest kind of protest and it really went deep! If you can get a little sex, too, then that added to the whole thing. It was like Wow! I'm saying no to war, no to racism, I mean--what a state!

MI: Did you have the impression that what happened when people--I mean, George and Roger--did you have the impression that what happened was what you expected?

CHARTERS: No. I must say, it was so different, and it has even changed so much in the last 40 years, that I can't go back to what was there in the 50s. We are so far from the isolation and the complete suppression that was there. What most people don't understand is that what happened to African-Americans was a dual experience: there was absolutely the physical repression of slavery and then the neo-slavery that followed and the police oppression. But people can rally from that. The other thing that happened was the continual, continual, denigration of the African-American as a human being: the entire entertainment world, the entire literary world, everything was saying over and over again "Man, you're nothin' but a fuckin' nigger, you can't do anything"--and this is what the African-American constantly had to fight against. They had the legacy of slavery and they'd say look at us! We fought free, but there was this total destruction of their own psyche, and this was what was going on. So, when I appeared in the ghetto I knew there was no way a single appearance few a few hours in a black boarding house in North Memphis was going to unravel a lifetime of...So, it was as complex for them as it was for me.

MI: So, in other words you didn't try to force them to call you Sam or something because it would've just been destructive.

CHARTERS: And also, they were going to have to face somebody else! I realized that when that sheriff came in to that house of Baby Tate's in Spartanburg--I realized that Annie and I were going to leave, but that sheriff was going to be right back, and Memphis Willie B. was going to have to deal with that. And there's a photograph--an incredibly poignant photograph--Annie took of them on the porch waiting for us to leave. Willie B.'s got this cigar holding his guitar and behind him is his wife holding the baby--and the anguish, and the apprehension in his eyes, knowing that we're about to get into the car and leave. And you never knew when the violence was going to come, and in what form. You just never knew.

I remember one time in New Orleans, we had those damn things in New Orleans where they had to--you know, the street cars they had these signs: "Colored Passengers Only," and you moved them up and down the street car and there were these slots so that you could always move the signs so that there were black people behind you. I remember the street car made the turn on Canal St. in about 1950 and a young black guy--the kind that whites were so terrified of--somehow bumped a white guy getting off the street car and instantly the guy started the whole thing: "You nigger what do you think you're doing!" and so on. And instantly that young black man was surrounded by whites--a mob instantly gathered. He dealt with it the only way he could, standing there saying "I'm sorry sir, I'm sorry sir," eyes on the ground. And after a moment, the crowd departed and they let him go.

I've been in little towns in Mississippi where there were fifteen white people on the one end of town and you could just feel the tension--the palpable tension--between them and the three hundred blacks who lived on the lower end of town where the streets were never paved, whereas up on the white end of town the streets were paved, there were the two cars. Just unbelievable! And there was no way I could pretend that I knew what it was like to grow up like that. There was no way I could say I understand it, understand the whites-- I didn't understand what it had done to the African-Americans. There was no way I could! And for me to pretend would just be ridiculous. I did a very specific thing which I hoped would somehow help to break down these barriers. But there was no way I could pretend they weren't there or that they were going to go away.

MI: With all that in mind, what did you think of some character like Elvis?

CHARTERS: Elvis was wonderful. Elvis was wonderful. He made absolutely no political thing whatsoever, just went into the army and was a great soldier. Did you ever read my book on Elvis?

MI: Did you write a book on Elvis!?

CHARTERS: I wrote a novel about Elvis. I've written two straight novels and then two musical novels: one is *Jelly Roll Morton's Last Night at the Jungle Inn*, where I use him to talk about jazz and what it has meant to the African-American community; and there's the one on Elvis, and it's *Elvis Presley Talks to His Mother After the Ed Sullivan Show*. Elvis did call his mother and they talked for three or four hours...So this is the phone call from the hotel room and it all draws on my experience traveling with rock and roll bands: Bill Haley and the Comets and Country Joe and the Fish, and all of what happens in hotel rooms after they play a gig. My book was a conscious strike at that damn book, that awful book by [Goldman]...There was a big biography that came out on Elvis about twenty years ago that just tore him to shreds and my book was an attempt to defend Elvis. Nobody read the book but there was one where I made up an incident of them being asked to play a party on their way down to do that Louisiana country show they did, and before they realize it--it's so dark--before they realize that it's a KKK party and people are saying to Elvis "Don't ya know nothin but this nigger shit?"

MI: So, you don't think of him--well, obviously you don't--but you don't think of him the way Elvis is presented...It's an expression of white people's racism that he is at all popular, etc. I mean, this is the really common these days."

CHARTERS: Go tell that to Ray Charles, Lionel Ritchie [laughs]...Elvis was--certainly, Bo Diddley always said that "He stole my stage act," but I've watched Bo Diddley's stage act, and come on, man! No, remember they had in '64--in '64 there was--I don't know if you know about that unbelievable Newport Folk Festival blues gathering, and I got to MC that program and that was heaven! I was hanging out in that old school house, they all were trading licks with each other, and afterwards they brought Hooker, Jimmy Reed, and the guy from Texas--T-Bone Walker to the Apollo for a blues night. Nobody came. I must say that Harlem stayed away by the millions...The few of us who were there, and these guys were awful! I mean, this was the Apollo and I was used to those R & B bands who just tore up the stage. And here was Jimmy Reed--T-Bone Walker went into his first act and his guitar fell off the stage! [laughs] Hooker couldn't find the plug to plug in his guitar! His back's to us while he's groping. He was so drunk that his son was playing with him and watching him hoping he wouldn't fall over. Here I was seeing the night of the blues at the Apollo Theater and it was just dreadful! So, Elvis didn't take any bread out of the mouths of these guys!...And anyone who was going to the Apollo Theater at that time is going to see James Brown. Is James Brown going to say that Elvis stole his stuff? What the heck is this? ...

MI: You said that you heard him [Elvis] in black neighborhoods?

CHARTERS: Oh yeah, all the time! They loved his music! Yeah, as I say, when I was canvassing for records around the South in black neighborhoods it was Gene Austin's "My Blue Heaven" that was the most common song I heard. That was Robert Johnson's big song! I mean, we created the blues singer, the black community didn't. They liked a whole range of music. Pop music--the function of pop music is to present the social mores involved with courting: how to deal with disappointment, how to deal with all this, and the blues presents only a tiny range of that. As I said, for me, as I told you before, that the ads in the newspapers featured the minstrel show stereotypes--the thick lips and all that--until the Mills Brothers. The Mills Brothers appeared in '29 and it was never the same...What we really forget is that Elvis didn't perform. He performed for two years then he went into the Army. He performed mostly in the South, he did a few television programs, he went into the Army, then he made movies. He didn't perform for fourteen years, or something like that. Then he did that TV show of him in his black suit --"

MI: And he was stoned!

CHARTERS: --and he kept saying "It's hot in this place!" [laughs] He was a lot of fun, then he disappeared to Las Vegas! He didn't really--I mean, to accuse Elvis of being anything but a straight guy who loved his mother too much is--but, he was so there, and he was enormously talented! I mean, you put "Jailhouse Rock" on--the wonderful moments in the auditoriums out there--the Avalon, the Fillmore--during the shows in the 60s during the acid days, they would have these light shows and part of the light shows was often movies. I remember in the Avalon Ballroom for a couple of weeks they were showing Elvis' "Jailhouse Rock" as part of the entertainment, and he was so much better than any of these people who were performing that they finally, discretely, stopped showing "Jailhouse Rock." They couldn't have those groups who were following the Grateful Dead at that time following Elvis! The dancing, the charisma of that guy! ...I think Elvis, until he disappeared into drugs, was basically a pretty decent guy.

MI: I read this thing--someone has published a book a few years ago, a couple of British guys, on Sun Records, and it was a wonderful book precisely because it started out how old Sam Phillips was the son of a share-cropper, loved Howlin' Wolf, and he loved a few of these other guys like Joe Hill Louis--Joe Louis Hill?--you know, just a few of these bluesmen that he actually wanted to record first, and he found he couldn't make a living at it, but he found someone who could play as well as they could, that he's not just a white guy, but a Southern guy who understands the music. It never even occurred to me to think of it that way...It's interesting to know that he [Elvis] was appreciated before by black audiences.

CHARTERS: Well, it's a--it swings the other way. You listen to his version of the Sleepy John Estes song he did, and I remember some guy saying "People said he took this from the black source, so I'm going to play the black original record and then I'm going to play Elvis' version," and there was no similarity! We couldn't hear anything in Elvis' version except the tremor. But what people don't remember is that Elvis' first big hit is "Love Me Tender"; that he did not have a big hit until he began singing the slow ballads. The other stuff he was doing was too black for the white audiences. They were not going to buy him doing a version of black stuff--they knew it. I mean, people are always listening vaguely to things and they turn off 90% if it, so they were aware that Negro music was there, and here was a white guy performing it. They didn't like it either. It was not until he did "Heartbreak Hotel" and "Love Me Tender," which he sang on this TV show and was his first big hit. The others were local hits. I heard the Sun records on black jukeboxes on Jerome St. in New Orleans; I didn't hear them in the white neighborhoods. He was too black. And the fact that he went through this--as I say, he tried to sing hillbilly ballads first--what? "Blue Moon of Kentucky"? He tried some of that stuff, too. The same with Bill Haley. I worked with Bill; I was Bill's producer for all those years. Bill just wanted to sing country music! [laughs] He had no idea that what he was doing was related to blacks at all, except he loved blacks a lot. It's just really, that his dream was to be Roy Rogers!

It is a shame, in a way, in that most of us who have done this writing were not Southerners, because Southerners know things that we don't know. And I hate to say something like this--I'm sure I told you about talking to Langston Hughes after the blues book came out and running one of these racist things by him, saying, you know--he's telling me what a great book it was, and we'd known each other for many years at Folkways, and I really liked Langston a lot--and I said to Langston, I ran this trip by you, I mean, a Negro would know much more about the blues than I do, he would have an understanding of this, you know. And then Langston looked at me and laughed and said "Tell me something I don't know about Schubert." [laughs] And it's absolutely true! What I was running through was just sentimental horse shit. I knew more about the blues than he did. I really did--in every way! It was the fact that he had dark skin, had grown up in Harlem, and how do you hear any blues in Harlem! I mean, what was all this crap about? ...

MI: There's another thing I was thinking about is that something I was peeking at was becoming slightly hysterical that you recorded Lightnin' Hopkins on an acoustic guitar and that this is trying to put him back on the plantation and all this kind of stuff. Was your decision to record him with an acoustic guitar--you know, what they keep saying is that this is a desire for purity, it's anachronistic...[part of discussion missing] That's what I think is interesting: people talk about your book, *The Country Blues*, as the beginning of the blues revival, and I always think--there's something about when that book took place that is not like what followed in a lot of ways. You know, like what happened five years later with all the revival concerts and so on. There's a gap.

CHARTERS: Yeah, I opened the door and went through it and what came out of it I could not have anticipated, nor was I even concerned. I was simply trying to preserve and represent this moment of American life. It was the same reason I was recording Charles Ives! And the same reason Annie was slaving over getting the first right recordings of Scott Joplin. Her first book is a biography of Bert Williams, the first black performer on the American stage. I mean, we were committed, but we were committed to something larger.

MI: You weren't trying to revive blues in the minds of people --

CHARTERS: I was trying to save America! [laughs] I mean, I was--of course I was pleased, I had a good time with the blues--but when the two albums I did of the Charles Ives violin and piano sonatas won all the best awards as among the top ten classical recordings of the year I was very excited. I was so excited! And when I was able to set up the thing at Utah State University so that for the first time in public there was a concert where there was a performance of sections of Scott Joplin's ragtime opera --

MI: The first time?

CHARTERS: The first time, in 1965, in Logan, Utah...So, the blues was magnificent, it was wonderful, but geez, there was a lot going on.

MI: I guess you could say that the stuff you liked in blues you found elsewhere also in many ways.

CHARTERS: Well, I like folk music, too, I mean, Doc Boggs and Doc Watson.

MI: There's something about how it's expressed there and what is expressed and who's doing it.

CHARTERS: I got a lot of flak when I moved--when in the 60s I began recording Country Joe and the Fish. No one had understood that what I was trying to initiate was a creative process, not a museum process, and working with Country Joe to create something new out of all the folk materials--I played five-string banjo for years. I appeared at the first Shakey's pizza parlor playing a five-string banjo and singing Woody Guthrie. So, I did the whole thing. So suddenly with Country Joe, he wanted to do the whole thing, too, but he couldn't figure out quite how to do it, and then we were putting together those first couple of albums. That, for me, was a totally logical understanding--you know, it seemed totally natural to me. I got a lot of flak! Magazine articles, you know, saying he sold out, you know. I didn't sell out! Man, they didn't know how hard it was to work with Country Joe! I would do an album with Lightnin' Hopkins--and an album with Lightnin' Hopkins took an hour and a bottle of gin--and all the incredible praise I got. For the second Country Joe, I worked six fuckin' months with those assholes and no one would even mention it! I was getting all this praise for--I did an album with Big Joe Williams in 40 minutes! That's all it took. C'mon Joe, sit down, he sang me a song, once you get the guitar in tune and keep it in tune the rest of it is--and yet people were carrying on so, like--I did so little! This had to be documented.

MI: It's interesting how you can be attacked for doing those people acoustically then get attacked for selling out for --

CHARTERS: As I say, as soon as you're in the way of somebody's view of themselves, of the importance of their role, nothing is easy! Unfortunately--in the arts, there is no zero sum in the arts. There can be any number of great blues singers, there can be any number of great poets--but to be the one great critic--there can only be one, so that if you are the person who is perceived as the one, then everyone will simply tear you down because you are the one! They can't take a place beside you as the other great one. So, this is why presidential elections are the way they are--there can only be one great president. If you want to be president, you'll do anything, say anything. But if you want to be a great poet, great poets know each other and they all like each other a lot. Joseph Brodsky would meet Seamus Heaney and they didn't get snippy at each other! [laughs] None of that shit goes on. And the artists on the lower East Side in the 50's inventing Abstract Expressionism, there was none of this crap going on about picking at each other! They were just saying "Wow, look at that!" [laughs] So, as you can see, this doesn't matter."

APPENDIX A

Roger Brown's Interview With Furry Lewis, Memphis, TN, C. 1970

An interview with Furry Lewis was often not so much an interview as a performance, an opportunity to tell some funny stories and some factually ambiguous anecdotes about his place in blues history. This interview is vintage Furry:

Roger Brown: Furry, tell me a little about when you used to play for the medicine shows.

Furry Lewis: Oh, it been many years ago, now. I'm old now--when I played in the medicine shows I wasn't as old I am now--77 years old. We used to play with a medicine show and we sold Jack Rabbit medicine. Travel Arkansas, Mississippi, Louisiana--we traveled quite a distance, played nice shows and sold nice medicine.

R.B.: Who were some of the people who played with you on those shows?

F.L.: We had a fellow there they called Cream Cheese, Jim Jackson, and a fellow they called Funny Willie--his name was Willie Polk--and a fellow they called Ham, and he played in my jug band, the Memphis Jug Band. He blowed the jug.

R.B.: Tell us something about the days when you played with the Memphis Jug Band.

F.L.: Oh, when I played in them days with the Memphis Jug Band, mostly what we did was serenading. Just like you be at your home and we knowed you and everything and we came, two or three o'clock in the morning. We get right out on your porch and we just break out and commence and start to playing music; and you and your wife would get up and start cooking and drinking coffee and everything else, in them days. Well, there was a jug band and I played with W. C. Handy, I played with Texas Alexander, I played with Memphis Minnie, Bessie Smith and Blind Lemon Jefferson. I played with each one I called.

R.B.: Tell me about when you met Blind Lemon.

F.L.: Oh, when I met Blind Lemon I was in Chicago. When I met Blind Lemon, that was the 20s, and I had to go up there to broadcast for the Vocalian. I was on Wabash Street, there in the Brunswick-Blake Building. That's where they make pool tables and everything. And I was up there--and that's where I met him all the time, up there. And some time I'd make a recording, I didn't meet him then, but any time I met him, ya know, it's like he'd make a recording the same day, something like that we met.

R.B.: Could you reminisce a little bit about Frank Stokes?

F.L.: Oh yes, Frank Stokes was a regular. Frank Stokes was a real regular, because Frank Stokes always did live around here where I'm at in Memphis. He lived in (Orange Mountain?), about four--five miles apart, wasn't like from here to New York. I used to go over to Frank Stokes' house, he used to come to mine, we used to just sit down, we just done all our playing together. And anywhere we set, set on my front porch here on Leith, we set out on his front porch on (Buntin?), any time we'd sit together they'd see us, they come.

R.B.: How about Hambone Willie Newborn?

F.L.: Oh, he's another good fellow, but he wasn't a old-timer like we was. And if he was, he wasn't in our band. Since then I met a whole lot of them old-timers, but they wasn't with the Memphis Jug Band, they was with some other kind of band, like this and that.

R.B.: Mention a little bit about what the different jug bands were, like Jack Kelly's, Jed Davenport's, and maybe one or two little things about each one in the 20s or 30s, if you can.

F.L.: Well, I will--I can and I will. There wasn't no difference, in nary a jug band--this come down to the original Memphis Jug Band, all of us couldn't be together. Some travel east, some travel west, some travel south--and all like that. It's all just the Memphis Jug Band, because all of us originated down on Beale Street. And all of us come under Handy. It's just one jug band--there were so many of us--there were four corners of the world, and we just have four bands, didn't all go together 'cause there were too many of us.

R.B.: You mean somebody could record one time with Cannon's Jug Stompers, then with the Memphis Jug Band, maybe with Jack Kelly; there was no fixed number of members for a particular band?

F.L.: No--no, no...

R.B.: I see. Ah--anything else on old days on Beale--old days on Beale Street?

F.L.: Well, I'll tell you one thing: where all of us got our start, there was a place on Beale Street called Pee Wee's. And Pee Wee's place, that was something they called a road house, a saloon. Everything was open then. The place never did close, 'cause when the place was first open, it had night bouncers and day bouncers. The day bouncers would get off, the night bouncers would come in. And when Pee Wee's just opened up, they taken the key, and take it over to West Memphis, Arkansas, and put the key around a rabbit's neck and told the key to go--told the rabbit to go--and ain't seen the key, and couldn't lock the damn place up. [laughter]

R.B.: When did this jug blowing start? Who first started blowing the jug?

F.L.: Well, the first I ever knowed to blow a jug was Son Brimmer. Yeah, they call him Will Shade. Son Brimmer.

R.B.: He blew before Gus did?

F.L.: Well, yeah. Oh, Gus never was such a good jug blower. Blowed some--but Son Brimmer and Ham was the best I ever heard--Son Brimmer, he started the Memphis Jug Band. Gus is a banjo player as long as I known him. He's a banjo player--he can kind've pick a little on a guitar, but you want to go get Gus right, put him on the banjo.

R.B.: Did Hammie Nixon blow the jug? Hammie Nixon was up around Brownsville, wasn't he?

F.L.: He's up around Brownsville, up around Sleepy John Estes. I've been in Sleepy John Estes' house up in Brownsville.

R.B.: How 'bout a little more on Jim Jackson's Jamboree? Tampa Red and...Were you around with all of them?

F.L.: Oh, I've been around 'em, I don't know who's older, me or Jim Jackson; he may be a little older than me, but I think I was born before he was. We just had it. Now, Tampa Red, Jim Jackson--you know one thing, we wouldn't go nowhere without the other 'n.

R.B.: Uh-huh.

F.L.: No, if you was to want me to play tonight, and didn't want nobody but me, I wouldn't go if I couldn't take Tampa Red and Jim

Jackson. That's the way--that's the way we made our living. That's a hard, hard time. At that time, Hoover was president. And I remember that times got so hard--Hoover was president--I happened to walk up an alley one time and I see'd a rat sittin' on top of a garbage can eatin' an onion and cryin'! (laughter)

APPENDIX B

"Roger Brown, the Detective, and Charley Lincoln's Mugshot"

A couple of the most famous Atlanta bluesmen of the 1920s and early 1930s are Barbecue Bob and Laughing Charley Lincoln. As anyone interested in old blues knows, Barbecue Bob and Laughing Charley were actually the brothers Charley and Robert Hicks, who were born in rural Georgia's cotton country in 1900 and 1902, respectively. The boys learned to play guitar from bluesman Curley Weaver's mother and no doubt learned to sing in church, and they began playing music at parties and fish fries when they were still young men.

These two musicians began their brief recording careers in 1927 when a talent scout heard Bob singing at an Atlanta barbecue and recruited him to record such country blues standards as the wildly successful "Barbecue Blues" and "Mississippi Heavy Water Blues." Charley Lincoln soon recorded his own more modest – and melancholy--successes, "My Wife Drove Me from the Door" and "Hard Luck Blues." Bob and Charley also recorded a couple of songs together called, "It Won't Be Long Now" in 1927 and "Darktown Gamblin'" in 1930. The 1930 session was Laughing Charley's last and Barbecue Bob died in 1931. The two men receded from memory as the years past and musical tastes changed, though the old 78s of their recordings remained forgotten in closets all over the South for decades to come.

By the middle 1950s, something happened that would cause at least some people to take a new interest in musicians such as Bob and Charley. Atlantans Roger Brown and George Mitchell, for instance, had begun to move unwittingly across the lines of segregation as ten or twelve year-olds when they discovered rhythm-and-blues on the radio just spinning the dial after school. Ruth Brown and Little Richard made quite an impression on the boys, but they discovered something that made them drop R&B in amazement when they read

Samuel Charters' book *The Country Blues* (1959) as teenagers and listened to its fabulous accompanying LP on Folkways.

The scratchy and obscure old recordings on *The Country Blues*, including such classics as "Walk Right in" by Cannon's Jug Stompers and "Fixin' to Die" by Bukka White, immediately hooked Roger and George with their powerful combination of folk rawness and incredible musicianship. The boys wanted to hear as much of the music as they could, but the problem was that it was very hard to locate any other country blues records to listen to in the early 1960s. Yet, when the boys realized that Samuel Charters had spoken to Will Shade and Gus Cannon in Memphis only a few years earlier, it occurred to them that it wasn't out of the question that they could see their musical idols in person, as well.

I've written about Roger and George's youthful blues-chasing and bluesman-seeking in my book *Blues Discovery: Reaching Across the Divide*, including an interview with Samuel Charters in which he describes how he had hoped that *The Country Blues* would elicit just such a reaction in other researchers who could help him to document the mostly-forgotten world of blues and jazz in the earlier part of the 20th century.

Part of the fascination of blues for enthusiasts such as Roger and George was the search for more information about the men and women who played the music. When were they born, and where? What were their real names? How many records did they record? And, of course, what did they look like?

Pictures of Robert Hicks have been around for some time – especially notable is the promotional picture of Bob with his guitar standing by a pile of meat in his barbecue cook's costume.

Bob's brother Charley Hicks, however, was only a name and a voice in the 1960s, and fellow Atlantans Roger and George were intrigued by the possibility of finding out more about him. When George was in Chicago in 1963, he asked the bluesman Big Joe Williams (1903-1982) if he knew what had become of Charley Lincoln. George understood Joe to say that Charley Lincoln was in Carrollton, Georgia, and as soon as they were both in Atlanta, Roger and George borrowed the Brown family's '61 Impala – cautiously removing the Goldwater for President bumper sticker placed there by Roger's brother before entering black neighborhoods – and set out for Carrollton. Unfortunately, no one in Carrolton knew of Charley Hicks and the trail went cold.

It was a few years later that things picked back up. The Atlanta bluesman Buddy Moss (1914-1984) told Roger that Charley and Bob's sister, Willie Mae Jackson, lived not far from him on Corley Avenue. When Roger talked to Mrs. Jackson, he discovered that Charley Lincoln had died in the penitentiary at Cairo, Georgia, in 1963. Mrs. Jackson told Roger that Charley had been sent to prison in 1955 because he had murdered a stranger on the street after a Christmas Day argument; she also said that she had retained no picture of her black sheep brother. This was a disappointment, but from this information Roger hatched a new plan: if Charley had gone to prison, then maybe he could find his mug shot?

With this information in hand, Roger went to Atlanta's police headquarters off Decatur Street and made his pitch to a detective about obtaining a copy of Charley's mug shot. The detective, a gentlemanly sort of the old school, located Charley Hick's file and laid it open on his desk. He shook his head and said, "He had a bad record." Roger told the detective that he was interested in Hicks as a musician, and since Hicks was dead there should be no harm in releasing the picture. The detective was reluctant, of course. Then Roger mentioned that he had interviewed Charley's sister.

The detective asked, "What's his sister's name?"

Roger said, "Willie Mae Jackson."

"Where does she live?"

"38 Corley Ave."

The detective shrugged and and tossed the mug shot across his desk and told Roger not to spread it around. And that was how Laughing Charley Lincoln came to have a face:

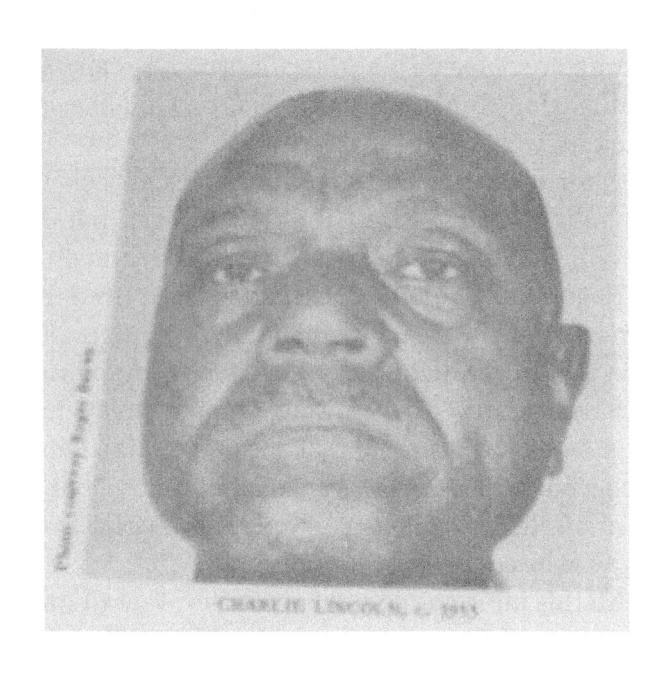

(Based on a phone interview with Roger Brown, 12/10/2011)

APPENDIX C

"A Talk With Peg Leg Howell Leads to News of Blind Willie McTell"

I wrote in a previous post about the youthful blues enthusiast Roger Brown's discovery of a photograph of the bluesman Laughing Charley Lincoln in the later 1960s--obtained by convincing an Atlanta police detective to give him the mug shot of Charley Hicks on file at the police station off Decatur Street. This was not the first time Roger had sought information on these nearly-forgotten musicians, however. Roger and his high school buddy, George Mitchell, had visited Will Shade, Charlie Burse, Gus Cannon, Furry Lewis, and Bo Carter in Memphis in 1962, and they had found Sleepy John Estes in the country near Brownsville not long after.

Roger Brown and Furry Lewis, Memphis, TN, c. 1970

After these remarkable experiences, Roger and George had also sought out information on the whereabouts of the Atlanta bluesman Blind Willie McTell, whose fabulous recordings of the 1920s and 30s, such as "Statesboro Blues," "Travelin' Blues," and "Broke-down Engine," are among the treasures of the recorded blues canon.

And the boys came close to what they hoped would be a lead on McTell when they found the bluesman Peg Leg Howell, who lived in the Summerhill section of Atlanta. As I put it in Blues Discovery: Reaching Across the Divide:

"In the Fall of 1962, Roger and George were freshmen at Emory University in Atlanta, but George had not stopped his blues activities at all. The fall of their freshman years the two of them were taking part in a fraternity rummage sale in Decatur, selling old clothes to poorer black people. The sale was set up in a vacant lot, and the patrons were blacks who were buying used clothes, not the middle classes, obviously. As they sold the clothes, the ever-alert George asked some of the people what they knew about local blues singers, and he was referred to a couple of guys Roger thinks were named Willie Roccomo and Clyde Upshaw, though he is unsure now.

"They went and spoke to Roccomo and Upshaw about singers who might still be around, and they told George that Peg Leg Howell, who had recorded a number of sessions from 1926 to 1930, was still alive. There was, again, the eighteen year-old's disbelief that a person already mature in the 1920s could still live in the 1960s. With this information, however, Roger and George, with their friend Jack Boozer, went down to Decatur Street in the heart of the black section of the city and walked into an old Decatur Street institution, Shorty's Barber Shop.

"When they went in, there were a couple of guys being served and a couple more waiting. One guy was having his hair straightened, another just a cut. They asked if anyone knew a musician named Peg Leg Howell, and a couple of them, a little guy and a big guy, immediately became animated, saying that they knew who he was. They had a discussion between each other--he's over there on such-and-such a street by so-and-so's house, right?--and they seemed to be thinking of a couple of different people. One of them finally said: 'No, no--Peg, you know, Peg!' and they seemed to come to an agreement.

"The two men led Roger and George over in Roger's car, finally turning down an alley and coming to a shabby one-story house in the thick of the slums. They walked up and knocked on the door, and a thin, faint voice said to come in. They walked in to the dark and dirty house, and there sat Peg Leg Howell on a wheelchair, legless and looking mighty old. They'd been warned that he had no legs, but the general poverty and signs of ill health were over-whelming."

Roger and George managed to spend time talking to Peg about his career and even to record an album of him playing and singing; and during their second meeting, Roger and George asked Peg if he had known Blind Willie McTell back in the old days – it never occurring to these young men that McTell could still be alive.

As they talked to Peg, a young guitarist from the neighborhood asked them, "That Blind Willie; did he play a 12 string guitar?"

"Yes," they said.

The young man shook his head confidently. "He ain't dead."

The boys sat straight up when they heard that. "He's not?!"

"He wasn't the last time I saw him."

"When was that?"

The young man considered. "Two years ago."

And thus began a wild ride up a variety of blind alleys. Among other things, Roger and George discovered that McTell had frequented the Blue Lantern on Ponce de Leon Ave. in the late 1950s, about two miles from Roger's house in Druid Hills; had they not been barely out of childhood then, he and George might have found McTell playing there for tips. The Blue Lantern also wasn't far from a restaurant called the Pig & Whistle, where John Lomax had had found McTell playing in 1940 and recorded the fabulous Library of Congress sessions in Lomax's hotel room.

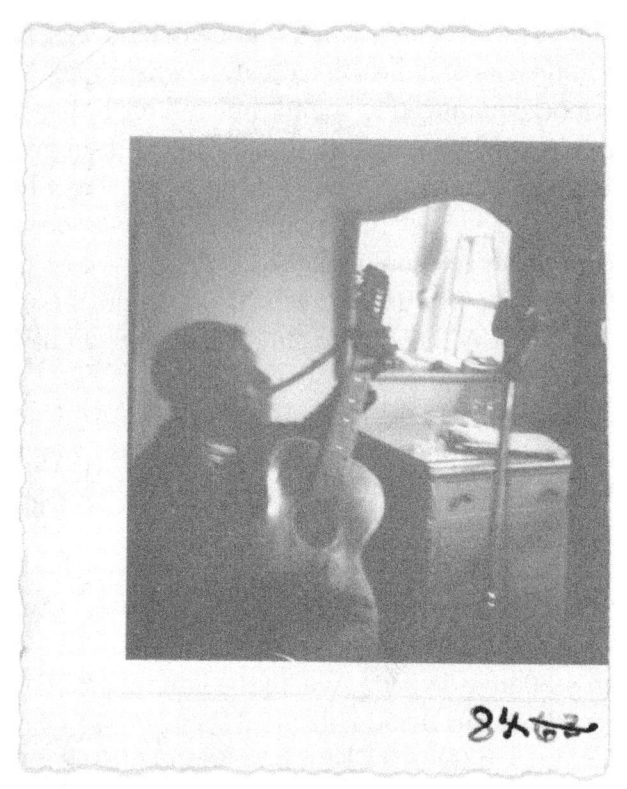

"Blind Willie McTell, with 12-string guitar, hotel room, Atlanta, Ga." (Library of Congress, http://lcweb2.loc.gov/service/pnp/ppmsc/00400/00400v.jpg)

Unfortunately, it wasn't long before Roger and George discovered that McTell had been dead since 1959. They'd missed him – but only just. As Roger recently told me, "Our uncanny luck running down Shade and Burse and later Estes was more the exception than the rule." They missed more musicians than they found. "Don't get me wrong: I'll never underestimate the blessing of our proximity to Buddy Moss and Robert Lockwood," and Roger only wishes he had been born a few years earlier…

(Based on a phone interview with Roger Brown, 12/10/2011

SELECT BIBLIOGRAPHY

INTERVIEWS

Matthew Ismail conducted interviews in 1995 and 1996 with Roger Brown in Durham, New Hampshire; Ray Flerlage in Chicago, Illinois; Bob Koester in Chicago, Illinois; and phone interviews with Samuel Charters and Fred Mendelsohn.

PUBLISHED SOURCES

Barlow, Bill, *Emergence of the Blues Looking Up at Down*. Temple University Press, 1989.

Bastin, Bruce, *Crying for the Carolines*. Studio Vista, 1971.

Bastin, Bruce, *Red River Blues: Blues Tradition in the South-East*. University of Ill. Pr, 1986.

Calt, Stephen, *I'd Rather Be the Devil: Skip James and the Blues*. Da Capo, 1994.

Calt, Stephen, *King of the Delta Blues...Charlie Patton*. Rock Chapel Press, 1988.

Charters, Samuel, *Robert Johnson*. Oak Publications, 1973.

Charters, Samuel, *Sweet as the Showers of Rain, The Bluesmen vol 2*. Oak Publications 1977.

Charters, Samuel, *The Bluesmen*. Oak Publications, 1967.

Charters, Samuel, *The Country Blues*. Michael Joseph, 1960.

Charters, Samuel, *The Legacy of the Blues*. Calder & Boyars, 1975.

Charters, Samuel, *The Poetry of the Blues*. Oak Publications, 1963.

Cohn, Lawrence, *Nothing But the Blues*. Abbeville press, New York 1993.

Collier, James Lincoln, *The Making of Jazz*. Dell Publishing, 1979.

Cook, Bruce, *Listen to the Blues*. Charles Scribner's Sons, 1975.

Davis, Francis, *The History of the Blues*. Hyperion, 1995.

Dixon & Godrich, *Blues and Gospel Records: 1890-1943*. Storyville, 1982.

Dixon & Godrich, *Recording the Blues*. Studio Vista, 1970.

Evans, David, *Big Road Blues: Tradition and Creativity in the Folk Blues*. Da Capo, 1982.

Evans, David, *Tommy Johnson*. Studio Vista, 1971.

Fahey, John, *Charlie Patton*. Studio Vista, 1971.

Ferris, William, *Blues From the Delta*. Studio Vista, 1971.

Garon, Paul, *Blues and the Poetic Spirit*. Edison Press, London, 1975.

Garon, Paul, *Woman with Guitar: Memphis Minnie's Blues*. Da Capo, 1992.

Garon, Paul & Beth, *The Devil´s Son in Law*. Studio Vista, 1971.

Guralnick, Peter, *Feel Like Going Home*. Outerbridge & Dienstfrey, 1971.

Guralnick, Peter, *Searching For Robert Johnson*. Dutton, 1989.

Heide, K G zur, *Deep South Piano*. Studio Vista 1970.

Keil, Charles, *Urban Blues*. University of Chicago Press, 1966.

Leadbitter, Mike, *Delta Country Blues*. Sussex: Blues Unlimited Publ, 1968.

Leadbitter, Mike, *Nothing But the Blues*. Hanover books, 1971.

Lieberman, Robbie. "*My Song Is My Weapon*" *People's Songs, American Communism, and the Politics of Culture, 1930-50*. U. of Illinois Press, 1995.

Lomax, Alan, *The Land Where the Blues Began*. The New Press, 1993.

Mitchell, George, *Blow My Blues Away*. Baton Rouge LSU Press, 1971.

Oakley, Giles, *The Devil´s Music: a History of the Blues*. Taplinger, 1977.

Obrechet, Jas, "The Atlanta Bluesmen: Barbecue Bob and Laughing Charley." *Jas Obrecht Music Archive* (http://jasobrecht.com/atlanta-bluesmen-barbecue-bob-laughing-charley-lincoln/)

Oliver, Paul, *Blues Fell This Morning: the Meaning of the Blues*. Horizon press, 1990.

Oliver, Paul, *Conversation With The Blues*. Cassel & Company, 1965.

Oliver, Paul, *Screening the Blues: Aspects of the Blues Tradition*. Cassel & Company, 1968.

Oliver, Paul, *Songsters and Saints*. Cambridge University Press, 1984.

Oliver, Paul, *Story Of The Blues*. Barrie & Rockliff, 1969.

Olsson, Bengt, Memphis Blues and Jug bands. Studio Vista, 1970.

Palmer, Robert, *Deep Blues*. Viking, 1981.

Ramsey, Frederick jr, *Been Here And Gone*. Rutgers, 1960.

Rowe, Mike, *Chicago Breakdown*. Da Capo, 1973.

Russell, Tony, *Blacks, Whites and Blues*. Studio Vista, 1970.

Santelli, Robert, *The Big Book of Blues*. Penguin 1993.

Wolfe, Charles, and Lornell, Kip. *The Life And Legend Of Leadbelly*. Harper Collins 1992.

ABOUT THE AUTHOR

Mathew Ismail is nothing if not curious. He has four Masters Degrees - ranging from Modern European Intellectual History to Islamic History--and has just published the revised edition of *Wallis Budge: Magic and Mummies in London and Cairo* (Dost Publishing, 2021), a book based on research in the archives of the British Museum, British Library, and Oxford University.

Matthew worked at universities in Dubai and Cairo from 1999-2011, which allowed him to get to know long-lost Syrian cousins and to travel throughout Europe, Africa, and Asia. His children were born in Abu Dhabi and Dubai and they grew up mostly in Cairo. Matthew now teaches meditation and yoga at Dost Meditation

https://www.dostpublishing.co/

Made in the USA
Middletown, DE
06 April 2025